TIMELINE OF THE
SIXTIES

what your dad was
up to when he
shoulda been
changin' yer
diapers!

Love, dad

TIMELINE OF THE
SIXTIES

GORDON KERR

canary
press

Omnipress Limited
Chantry House
22 Upperton Road
Eastbourne,
East Sussex BN21 1BF

© 2009 Omnipress Limited
www.omnipress.co.uk

This 2009 edition published by Canary Press,
an imprint of Omnipress Limited, UK

ISBN: 978-0-9537976-8-4

Printed and bound in China

10 9 8 7 6 5 4 3 2 1

COVER & INTERNAL DESIGN
Anthony Prudente on behalf of Omnipress Limited
Artworking by Vivian Foster

Contents

Introduction

At the beginning of the 1950s, the shadow of World War II still loomed large. Shortages and rationing were still in place as the world desperately tried to recover from six years of terrible strife. Towards the end of that gloomy decade, however, the forces that would shape the coming ten years were already being formed.

In Cuba, the corrupt Batista government fell in 1959, heralding the arrival of Fidel Castro as president, an event that made the United States uneasy and that would, in the early years of the coming decade, lead the world to the brink of what would undoubtedly have been a catastrophic nuclear war.

In America, the young US Senator, John F. Kennedy, was campaigning to replace Dwight D. Eisenhower as president of the United States, hoping to wipe away the last vestiges of World War II leadership and breathe new life into his country. Meanwhile, a young black preacher named Martin Luther King was visiting India, learning about Mahatma Gandhi's method of non-violent protest, while at a school in Little Rock, Arkansas, protests against the segregation of schools led to the calling out of the National Guard.

In 1959, in the United Kingdom, Harold Macmillan increased his majority in a general election, facing a term in office when the independence of countless African states would bring Britain's empire to an end. Meanwhile, in Liverpool, 17-year-old John Lennon had broken up his band, the Quarrymen, and he and 17-year-old Paul McCartney were writing songs in the hope that, one day, someone might listen to them.

The 1960s would be a decade of great change in the world; a decade of great political and social upheaval; a decade of optimism following the despair, depression and conflict of the first five decades of the 20th century; a decade of colour and excitement, of new music, new art and new fashions. It was also a decade that would bring previously undreamed of technological developments, culminating in a man standing on the surface of the Moon on 20 July 1969. There was still conflict, of course, but nothing, thankfully, on a global scale.

They used to say that if you can remember the sixties, you were not really there. Hopefully, this book will help to bring it all back to you, or introduce you to the tumultuous events of one of the modern world's most vibrant and exciting decades.

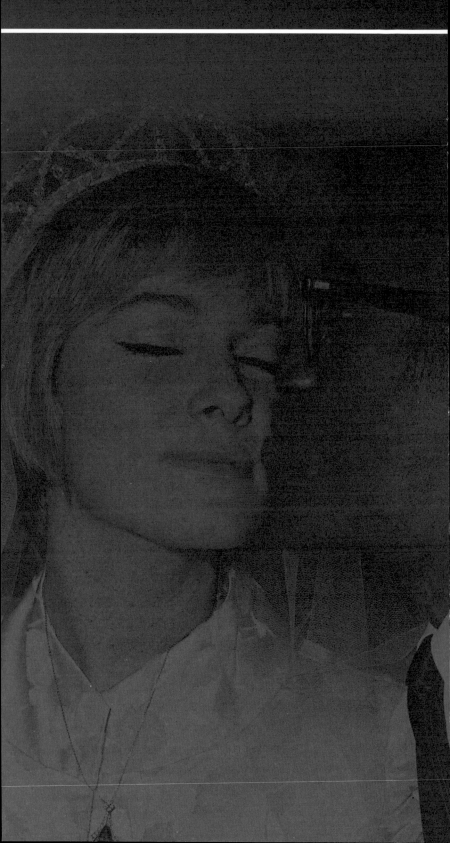

BRAVE NEW
WORLD

1960

January

The World The population of the world is more than 3 billion.

East Germany The first of 160,000 refugees cross from East Germany to West Germany following food shortages. Soviet premier Nikita Khrushchev orders the construction of a wall 165 km (103 miles) long and 3.6 m (12 ft) high with guards and barbed wire to stop the flow of refugees to the West.

Algeria There is a major insurrection against French colonial policy; President De Gaulle sacks Jacques Massu, commander-in-chief of the French forces in Algeria. The French government seizes copies of four newspapers that contain reports of terrible conditions in prison camps in Algeria.

Egypt The foundation stone for Egypt's Aswan High Dam is laid; the dam is being built to prevent the Nile from flooding, to generate electricity and to provide water for agriculture.

Cameroon gains independence from France.

Kenya The Mau Mau uprising – an insurgency begun in 1952 by rebels against British rule – ends in military failure for the rebels but hastens independence for Kenya. A parliamentary conference indicates that the British will accept 'one person, one vote' majority rule in the country.

Rwanda Rwandans vote, by referendum, with the support of the Belgian colonial government, to abolish the Tutsi monarchy and replace it with a republic; the Hutu, Dominique Mbonyumutwa, is the first president of the transitional government.

Belgian Congo A conference in Brussels culminates with the announcement of a date for independence, 30 June; national elections will take place in May.

South Africa 437 miners die in a rock fall at Coalbrook.

USA Massachusetts senator, John F. Kennedy, announces his candidacy for the Democratic presidential nomination.

Antigua and Barbuda Sir Vere Cornwall Bird Sr, leader of the Antiguan Labour Party, is elected chief minister; he has never received any formal education, apart from primary schooling.

Grenada Herbert Blaize, leader of the Granada National Party, is elected chief minister.

Vietnam The United States has given almost $2 billion in aid to South Vietnam; 685 non-combat advisors are currently stationed there.

Burma U Nu's 'Clean' faction of the Anti-Fascist People's Freedom League (AFPFL) wins a landslide victory over Ba Swe and Kyaw Nyein's 'Stable' faction and returns to power.

· ·

Entertainment: The US Army promotes Elvis Presley to sergeant. Lionel Bart's musical *Oliver!* is premiered in London.

Science & Technology: American physicist John Reynolds sets the age of the solar system at 4,950,000,000 years. The Bathysphere *Trieste*, with Jacques Piccard and Don Walsh on board, reaches the bottom of the Pacific at 10,900 metres – almost seven miles – east of the Philippines.

Died: Albert Camus, Nobel Prize-winning French writer, 46. Nevil Shute, British author, 60. Margaret Sullavan, US actress, 50.

· ·

February

United Kingdom Harold Macmillan makes his historic *Wind of Change* speech to the South African Parliament: the speech signals clearly that the British Government intends to grant independence to many African territories; he says, 'The wind of change is blowing through this continent. Whether we like it or not, this growth of national consciousness is a political fact';

he also makes clear the British Government's attitude to apartheid – '…it is our earnest desire to give South Africa our support and encouragement, but I hope you won't mind my saying frankly that there are some aspects of your policies which make it impossible for us to do this without being false to our own deep convictions about the political destinies of free men to which in our own territories we are trying to give effect.' Queen Elizabeth II confirms that she and her descendants will be known as the House and Family of Windsor, but that their personal surname, should one be needed, will be Mountbatten-Windsor.

France explodes its first atomic bomb in the Sahara desert, becoming the world's fourth nuclear power.

Denmark Social Democrat, Viggo Kampmann, becomes prime minister, heading a minority government with the Social Liberal Party.

Morocco 12,000 die in an earthquake that destroys the town of Agadir.

India 12 Indian soldiers die in border clashes with Chinese troops.

USA The first of the decade's historic civil rights protests begins when four black North Carolina students stage a sit-in at the lunch counter of a branch of Woolworth's in Greensboro, North Carolina; a young preacher, Dr Martin Luther King, is arrested during the Alabama bus boycott. Adolph Coors III, chairman of the Coors Brewing Company, is kidnapped in Golden, Colorado; he is later found dead; former Fulbright scholar, Joseph Corbett Jr is arrested for the murder after two Canadians recognize him from a *Reader's Digest* article; he is sentenced to life imprisonment.

DR MARTIN LUTHER KING

Dr Martin Luther King became pastor of the Dexter Avenue Baptist Church in Montgomery, Alabama, in 1954. He was always a dedicated worker for the civil rights movement. The following year he accepted the leadership of the first African-American nonviolent demonstration of contemporary times in the USA. The demonstration lasted for 382 days and during this time King was arrested, his home was bombed and he was subjected to personal abuse, but he never gave up his fight. King became the youngest man to receive the Nobel Peace Prize. When he was notified of the award, he announced that he would turn over the prize money of $54,123 (£33,317) to the furtherance of the civil rights movement.

Cuba President Fidel Castro puts all industry under government control. The Soviet Union agrees to buy 5 million tons of Cuba's sugar in the next five years and to supply Cuba with crude oil, petroleum products, wheat, iron, fertilizers and machinery; it also gives Cuba $100 million in credit at 2.5 per cent interest.

Chile The Valdivia earthquake kills around 6,000 and creates a tsunami affecting Chile, Hawaii, Japan, the Philippines, New Zealand, Australia and the Aleutian Islands in Alaska.

Cambodia At the second congress of the Workers' Party of Kampuchea, Pol Pot is elected the party's general secretary; he founds the Khmer Rouge which will become the governing party in years to come.

• •

Entertainment: Joanne Woodward receives the first ever star on the Hollywood Walk of Fame.

Science & Technology: The CERN particle accelerator is inaugurated at Geneva in Switzerland; it uses electric fields to propel electrically-charged particles to high speeds and to contain them.

Sport: The 8th Winter Olympics begin in Squaw Valley, California.

Born: Prince Andrew, second son of Queen Elizabeth II and Prince Philip; he is second in line to the British throne. Crown Prince Naruhito Hironomiya, eldest son of Emperor Akihito and heir to the Japanese throne.

Died Edwina Cynthia Annette Mountbatten, Countess Mountbatten of Burma, wife of the Lord Louis Mountbatten and last Vicereine of India, 58. Adriano Olivetti, Italian engineer and manufacturer, 58.

• •

March

United Kingdom 20 firefighters die in a fire at a whisky warehouse in Glasgow. The first Doc Marten 1460 boot is produced in Wollaston, Northamptonshire.

Switzerland The Canton of Geneva gives women the right to vote for the first time. Ten nations meet in Geneva to discuss nuclear disarmament.

East Germany Walter Ulbricht is elected chairman of the Council of State, effectively head of state.

South Africa Martial Law is declared following the Sharpeville Massacre; in the township of Sharpeville police shoot dead 72 people protesting about the Pass Laws introduced in 1923 to regulate the movement of black Africans in urban areas; the ANC (African National Congress) is outlawed; a state of emergency is declared when 50 more black people are killed. The PAC (Pan Africanist Congress) announces a campaign against the Pass Laws and 50,000 demonstrate against them in the township of Langa; ANC leader, Albert Luthuli is arrested and imprisoned for five months for publicly burning his pass following Sharpeville; other ANC leaders, including Nelson Mandela, also burn theirs. Mandela is appointed leader of the African National Congress's armed wing, Umkhonto we Sizwe.

Iraq 30 men are executed after an attack on President Abd al-Karim Qasim.

Ceylon Dudley Senanayake, leader of the United National Party, is elected prime minister; it is the second of his three terms as head of the government.

USA Civil rights protests continue when 1,000 black students pray and sing the national anthem on the steps of the old Confederate Capitol building in Montgomery, Alabama. President Eisenhower approves the assembling of an anti-Cuban army of exiles under the control of the CIA, to be prepared for action against the new Castro government. The president announces that 3,500 US troops will be sent to Vietnam to support the Diem regime. The US appeals court rules that D. H. Lawrence's novel, *Lady Chatterley's Lover,* is not obscene.

Cuba Fidel Castro blames America for an explosion on board a French cargo ship, *La Coubre,* while its cargo of 76 tons of Belgian weapons is being unloaded at Havana; 136 people die; some sources claim that it is an act of sabotage carried out on the orders of the CIA by William Alexander Morgan, an American citizen who fought for Castro in the Cuban Revolution. Cuban photographer Alberto Korda takes the picture of Che Guevara at a rally that becomes a symbol of the Cuban revolution and one of the most famous poster and t-shirt images of all time.

• •

Entertainment: Elvis Presley ends his two-year spell in the US Army. US TV and film star Lucille Ball divorces Desi Arnaz.

Medicine & Health: In Seattle, Clyde Shields is implanted with the first kidney dialysis shunt; he lives a further 11 years; developed in 1940, the dialysis process has previously been restricted to operating theatres.

Science & Technology: *Pioneer 5* is launched into solar orbit between Earth and Venus by the USA. The first guided missile is launched from the US nuclear submarine, the USS *Halibut.*

Sport: The Chicago Cardinals baseball franchise moves to St Louis.

Born: Adam Clayton, British-Irish bass player (U2). Ivan Lendl, Czechoslovakian tennis player. Ayrton Senna, Brazilian racing driver.

Died: Joseph Haas, German composer, aged 81.

• •

April

United Kingdom The ballistic missile, the *Blue Streak,* is cancelled; it is not credible as a nuclear deterrent; its liquid oxygen fuel ices up and consequently has to be loaded immediately prior to use; this takes 15 minutes by which time enemy damage would be done; the rocket is used as the first-stage of the European satellite launcher *Europa* until 1972.

France explodes two atom bombs in the Sahara. Four-year-old Eric Peugeot, youngest son of the founder of the car company, is kidnapped; he is released on payment of a ransom of around £50,000 ($82,000); Pierre Larcher and Raymond Rolland are arrested and charged with the kidnapping. President de Gaulle narrowly escapes assassination.

Austria Alfons Gorbach of the Austrian People's Party is elected chancellor of Austria.

Sweden ordains its first three women priests.

Togo gains independence from France; Sylvanus Olympio becomes its first chief of state.

South Africa While giving a speech to mark the jubilee of the Union of South Africa, Prime Minister Henrik Verwoerd is shot twice in the face by a 52-year-old farmer, David Pratt – Pratt is an anti-apartheid activist and fervent advocate of South Africa remaining in the British Empire. Verwoerd returns to public life less than two months after the shooting; this incident, plus the *Winds of Change* speech made by Harold Macmillan, helps Verwoerd to persuade white South Africans that the country should go it alone and declare itself a republic. In the Unlawful Organizations Act, membership of the African National Congress (ANC) and the Pan Africanist Congress (PAC) is punishable by imprisonment; the ANC will remain banned until 1990.

Tibet The Dalai Lama appeals to Asian and African countries to help his people.

Malaya Tuanku Abdul Rahman dies; Hisamuddin Alam Shah replaces him as Yang di-Pertuan Agong – head of state.

USA The US Senate passes a landmark Civil Rights Bill; it establishes federal inspection of local voter registration polls and introduces penalties for anyone who obstructs an attempt to register to vote or to actually vote. The CIA begins planning the disastrous 1961 Bay of Pigs invasion of Cuba.

Cuba buys oil from the USSR.

Brazil Brasilia, the new capital, is inaugurated; the seat of national government is transferred there from Rio de Janeiro.

Paraguay President Stroessner announces the defeat of an invasion by armed rebels.

South Korea President Syngman Rhee's government is toppled amid accusations of a rigged election; an enquiry begins into summary executions during the Korean War; Rhee is whisked out of the country on board a plane operated by Civil Air Transport – an airline owned by the CIA; he takes with him $20 million of embezzled funds.

Burma U Nu is elected prime minister for a third time.

• •

Entertainment: American rock star, Eddie Cochran, dies when the taxi in which he is travelling through Chippenham in England, crashes into a lamppost; fellow passenger, singer Gene Vincent is seriously injured, but survives.

Science & Technology: The United States launches *TIROS 1*, the first weather satellite. The first underwater launch of a Polaris missile is carried out successfully.

Born: Rafael Benitez, Spanish football coach. Jeremy Clarkson, British broadcaster and journalist. Linford Christie, British athlete. Roger Taylor, British musician (Duran Duran). Paula Yates, British television presenter.

Died: Eddie Cochran, US singer, 21. Tuanku Abdul Rahman ibni Almarhum Tuanku Muhammad, Malaya's first head of state, 64.

• •

May

Europe United Kingdom, Ireland, Denmark and Norway apply for membership of the European Community; French president de Gaulle vetoes the applications. The European Free Trade Association (EFTA) is founded as an alternative trade bloc for nations not admitted into the EEC; Britain, Austria, Denmark, Norway, Portugal, Sweden, Portugal and Switzerland are members.

United Kingdom Princess Margaret, sister to the Queen, marries a commoner, the photographer Anthony Armstrong-Jones at Westminster Cathedral.

USSR Leonid Brezhnev becomes president. An American U-2 spy plane piloted by Francis Gary Powers is shot down near Sverdlovsk; Powers is held captive for 21 months; Premier Nikita Khrushchev demands an apology from President Eisenhower and brings to an abrupt end the Big Four summit meeting involving France, Britain, the USA and the USSR, in Paris, on account of the incident.

Turkey A military coup by 37 army officers ousts the government of Adnan Menderes; he and other party members are arrested, charged with violating the constitution and sentenced to death; General Cemal Gürsel takes over.

Morocco King Muhammad V becomes head of government.

USA Senator John F. Kennedy wins a Democratic Party primary in West Virginia. Caryl Chessman, convicted robber and rapist, is executed in the gas chamber at San Quentin. UN Ambassador Henry Cabot Lodge accuses the Russians of concealing a microphone inside a wooden carving of the Great Seal of the United States that they have presented to the United States embassy in Moscow.

Mexico Ramon Mercader, murderer of Leon Trotsky in 1940, is freed from prison after serving 20 years; he lives the remainder of his life in Cuba and the USSR where he is awarded the country's highest accolade, the Hero of the Soviet Union medal.

Argentina There is jubilation in Israel when Nazi war criminal, Adolf Eichmann, is captured by Israeli agents in Buenos Aires while returning home from work at a Mercedes factory.

Chile One of the greatest earthquakes on record causes tsunamis in every coastal town between the 36th and 44th parallels; 1,000 die; beaches in Hawaii are devastated and its effects are felt as far away as the Japanese coast.

Paraguay The country's celebration of 150 years of independence is disrupted by anti-government demonstrations; police respond with brutal beatings and arrests of students.

India Bombay state is split into Gujurat and Maharashtra.

Taiwan Chiang Kai-shek, president since 1950, is re-elected; he will remain president until his death in 1975.

Japan Socialist members of the Diet, the Japanese Parliament, are removed by force amidst protests during a debate about a security treaty with the United States; the Diet approves the treaty.

· ·

Entertainment: Jean Genet's *Le Balcon* premieres in Paris. DJ Alan Freed who coined the term 'rock 'n' roll' is accused of bribery in a radio payola scandal in America; he is found to have accepted money and gifts to play records and loses his job.

Medicine & Health: In the United States, the pill Enovid is approved for use as the first oral contraceptive; made by G. D. Searle & Co of Chicago, the research into the pill has been mostly funded by farm machinery heiress and women's rights activist, Katherine McCormick.

Science & Technology: The USS *Triton* completes the first underwater circumnavigation of the globe; it has taken 54 days. US Air Force Major, Robert M. White flies the X-15 plane to a height of 33,222 m (108,996 ft).

Sport: In one of the most unforgettable matches in football history, Real Madrid memorably defeat Eintracht Frankfurt 7-3 to win the European Cup in front of 135,000 at Hampden Park, Glasgow.

Born: Paul Hewson (Bono), Irish singer (U2). Jeffrey Dahmer, US serial killer. Yannick Noah, French tennis player and singer.

Died: Boris Pasternak, Russian writer and poet, 70. John D. Rockefeller, US philanthropist, 86.

· ·

June

East Germany First Secretary of the Socialist Unity Party and GDR State Council Chairman, Walter Ulbricht, states at an international press conference, 'No one has the intention of erecting a wall!'

Italy Police ruthlessly suppress demonstrations against support by Fernando Tambroni's Christian Democrat government for the Neo-Fascist Italian Social Movement that had been founded by supporters of former dictator, Benito Mussolini, after World War II.

USSR In an address to the United Nations, Prime Minister Khrushchev pledges his country's support for 'wars of national liberation'.

Algeria Fighting continues as the National Liberation Front agrees to peace talks in Paris.

Democratic Republic of the Congo After the former Belgian Congo gains independence from Belgium, Patrice Lumumba forms the newly independent nation's first government; civil war breaks out; a sub-committee of the US National Security Council authorizes the assassination of Lumumba.

Madagascar (formerly Malagasy Republic) gains independence from France. Philibert Tsiranana, leader of the moderate Social Democratic Party is president; he creates an authoritarian one-party state.

Mali gains independence from France as the Mali Federation. Modibo Keita is the first president; he leads his country towards the progressive socialization of the economy.

Somali Republic British Somaliland gains independence from Britain and five days later unites with Italian Somaliland and French Somaliland to form the Somali Republic.

USA stops the import of sugar from Cuba. Senator John F. Kennedy wins the California Democratic primary. Alfred Hitchcock's *Pyscho* opens in New York.

❝ A man may die, nations may rise and fall, but an idea lives on. ❞

John F. Kennedy

Cuba US oil companies in the country refuse to refine Soviet oil.

China launches its first ballistic missile. Typhoon Mary kills 1,000 in Fukien province.

Taiwan The disputed island of Quemoy is hit by 500 artillery shells fired from the Chinese coast; during this period the steel of the shells fired from China becomes a natural resource for the local economy; Quemoy becomes famous for producing cleavers from it.

Japan 182 students are arrested in violent demonstrations at Tokyo University over the security treaty with the United States; Prime Minister Nobusuke Kishi resigns and an election is called.

New Zealand has its first television transmission.

Entertainment: The Beatles change their name from the Silver Beatles to the Beatles for their first professional engagement at the Neston Institute.

Science & Technology: The British radio telescope at Jodrell Bank in Cheshire sets a new space record when it makes contact with the *Pioneer V* satellite at a distance of 36.2 million km (22.5 million) miles.

Born: Mick Hucknall, British singer (Simply Red). John Taylor, British musician (Duran Duran). John Elway (quarterback Denver Broncos).

Died: Lottie Dod, British tennis player, 88.

July

Europe The Organization for Economic Co-operation and Development is founded, based in Paris and supporting the principles of representative democracy and free-market economy.

United Kingdom At a party at Cliveden, home of Viscount Astor, secretary of state for war in Harold Macmillan's Conservative government. John Profumo, meets model and callgirl, Christine Keeler and the two begin an affair.

The Profumo Affair was a political scandal named after the then secretary for war, John Profumo. It began when Profumo had a brief relationship with a callgirl named Christine Keeler. The affair would probably have gone unnoticed had it not been for the fact that Keeler was also reputedly the mistress of a known Russian spy. When Profumo was questioned about this matter in the House of Commons he blatantly lied and the scandal forced him to resign. This affair also severely damaged the reputation of Harold Macmillan's government, and he himself resigned a few months later.

Italy Christian Democrat, Amintore Fanfani is elected prime minister for the third time.

USSR Premier Nikita Khrushchev threatens to use rockets to protect Cuba from the United States. A six-man US reconnaissance plane is shot down over the Soviet Union; the two surviving officers are imprisoned in Moscow's feared Lubyanka prison. Captured US pilot, Gary Powers, pleads guilty to espionage charges.

Iran recognizes Israel to the displeasure of the Arab League; Egypt shuts down its embassy in Tehran.

Ghana Kwame Nkrumah is elected first president of the new Republic of Ghana, independent since 1957.

Democratic Republic of the Congo Katanga province, led by Moise Tshombe and supported by Belgian interests and troops, breaks away from the new government of Patrice Lumumba; the United Nations sends troops to supervise the withdrawal of Belgian troops. Belgium announces that it believes the trouble in its former colony is the result of a communist plot.

USA John F. Kennedy wins the Democratic Party's presidential nomination in Los Angeles; Vice-President Richard M. Nixon wins at the Republican convention in Chicago. Elijah Muhammad, leader of Nation of Islam, calls for a black state. The Woolworth's lunch-counter in Greensboro, North

Carolina, scene of a sit-in by four African Americans in February, serves its first black customer. Los Angeles Psychiatrist, Sidney Cohen's survey of 5,000 people who have taken LSD, concludes that the drug is safe.

Cuba Fidel Castro nationalizes US-owned Esso, Shell and Texaco facilities as well as all US-owned sugar refineries.

Guatemala 225 die in a fire in an asylum in Guatemala City.

Ceylon Dudley Senanayake's coalition collapses; following fresh elections, Sirimavo Bandaranaike, leader of the Sri Lanka Freedom Party, becomes the world's first elected female head of government; she is the widow of the previous prime minister, Solomon Bandaranaike, who was assassinated by a Buddhist monk in 1959.

Malaya Hisamuddin Alam Shah declares the end of the 12-year-long 'emergency'.

Japan Liberal Democrat Hayato Ikeda is elected prime minister; he is later described as 'the single most important figure in Japan's rapid growth… the man who pulled together a national consensus for economic growth.'; he is re-elected in December 1960 and December 1964.

South Vietnam More than 60,000 Buddhists protest against the government of President Ngo Dinh Diem.

Cambodia Pol Pot is on a list of 34 leftists who are summoned by King Norodom Sihanouk to join the government and to declare loyalty to him; Pol Pot and his associate Chou Chet refuse and leave Phnom Penh to establish an insurgent base in Tatanakri Province in the north-east of the country.

Science & Technology: US physicist Theodore Maiman introduces the first working laser, beating several other teams also working towards it.

Sport: The USSR defeats Yugoslavia to win the first European Football Championship. Yachtsman Francis Chichester, aboard *Gypsy Moth II*, sets a record of 40 days for a solo crossing of the Atlantic.

Born: Ian Hislop, British satirist.

Died: Aneurin Bevan, Welsh Labour politician, 62. German Field Marshal Albrecht von Kesselring, aged 74.

August

East Germany On 12 August, East German leaders attend a garden party in Dollnsee, north of East Berlin; there, East German leader, Walter Ulbricht, signs the order to close the border between East and West Berlin and to erect a wall separating the two halves of the city. At midnight, police and East German troops close the border, they begin to tear up the streets that run along it so that they cannot be used by vehicles. 156 km (97 miles) of barbed wire and fences are installed along the border's length and around the three western enclaves. On 15 August, the first concrete elements begin to be added; during the work, soldiers are stationed along its entire length with orders to shoot anyone trying to cross to the West; during the 28 years and one day of the wall's existence, more than 200 people will die trying to escape to West Berlin.

Cyprus gains independence from Britain; Archbishop Makarios, archbishop and primate of the Cypriot Orthodox Church, political leader since 1959, is its first president.

USSR withdraws all advisors, aid and other support from China. US pilot Gary Powers goes on trial and is convicted of espionage; he is sentenced to 10 years imprisonment.

Democratic Republic of the Congo Demonstrations break out against the Lumumba government.

Republic of the Congo formerly Congo/Brazzaville, (not to be confused with the Democratic Republic of Congo), declares independence from France; former priest, Fulbert Youlou, is elected the country's first president.

Dahomey gains independence from France with Hubert Maga as president.

Upper Volta formerly part of French West Africa, gains independence under Maurice Yaméogo; in 1984 it will be renamed Burkina Faso.

Chad gains independence from France but remains within the French community; teacher and trade union activist François Tombalbaye is the first head of government.

Central African Republic gains independence from France, with David Dacko as the country's first president.

Côte D'Ivoire Former village chief, Félix Houphouët-Boigny, becomes the first president of the newly independent nation; it is West Africa's most prosperous country, responsible for 40 per cent of the region's exports.

Gabon gains independence from France with Leon M'ba as its first president.

Senegal leaves the Mali Federation due to political differences and declares independence.

USA Students stage kneel-in demonstrations in churches in Atlanta; a race riot breaks out in Jacksonville, Florida. CIA officials approve a number of plans to assassinate Fidel Castro, president of Cuba.

Ecuador José María Velasco Ibarra is elected president for the fourth of five times.

South Korea Following the ousting of Syngman Rhee by a student-led pro-democracy uprising in April, Yun Bo-seon becomes president; he is merely a figurehead as the authoritarian nature of Rhee's administration has led to the introduction of a parliamentary system.

Laos Kong Le leads a bloodless military coup. Prime Minister Prince Somsanith, resigns and King Sri Savang Vatthana names Souvanna Phouma prime minister. Kong Le declares the coup over and withdraws from the council of ministers.

• •

Entertainment: Chubby Checker launches a new dance craze with 'The Twist'. The Beatles make their debut in Hamburg with Stuart Sutcliffe on bass and Pete Best on drums. The satirical review *Beyond the Fringe* starring Dudley Moore, Peter Cook, Alan Bennet and Jonathan Miller, premieres at the Edinburgh Festival.

Medicine & Health: The first oral contraceptive pill is sold in Skokie, Illinois.

Science & Technology: US Air Force Major Joseph H. Engle increases his height record to 41,600 metres (55.9 miles) in the X-15 rocket-powered plane. The first balloon satellite, *Echo 1*, is launched from Cape Canaveral; it enables the first two-way telephone conversation by satellite. Flying in a hot-air balloon, US test pilot Joe Kittinger reaches the highest altitude ever by a man in non-powered flight (31 km/19.3 miles) and becomes the first man to exceed the speed of sound without an aircraft or space vehicle when he parachutes back to Earth. The USSR launches the *Sputnik 5* spaceship; on board are the dogs Belka and Strelka, 40 mice, two rats and a number of plants; all are safely recovered after a day in space; the dogs, mice and rats are the first animals to survive orbital flight.

Sport: The 17th Olympic Games open in Rome; Ethiopian marathon runner, Abebe Bikila, becomes the first African to win an Olympic track and field gold medal.

Born: Antonio Banderas, Spanish actor. Sarah Brightman, British singer. David Duchovny, US actor. Timothy Hutton, US actor. Branford Marsalis, US jazz musician. Sean Penn, US actor and director. Kenny Perry, US golfer.

Died: Oscar Hammerstein II, US librettist 65. Vaino Hannikainen, Finnish composer, 60.

••

September

The World The International Development Association (IDA) is founded by the World Bank to provide long-term, interest-free loans to the world's 81 poorest countries.

United Nations 15 new African nations are admitted.

United Kingdom publisher Penguin Books is charged with obscenity for trying to publish D. H. Lawrence's racy novel *Lady Chatterley's Lover.*

France The far-right nationalist militant organization the OAS (*Organisation de l'Armée Sécrète*) make an unsuccessful attempt to assassinate President de Gaulle; it is a last-ditch effort to save Algeria for France.

West Germany Konrad Adenauer elected to serve a fourth term as chancellor.

East Germany further limits access to East Berlin for West Berliners.

Democratic Republic of the Congo President Kasa-Vubu, angered by Prime Minister Patrice Lumumba's soliciting of Soviet involvement in the country, dismisses Lumumba with the support of America's CIA and places him under house arrest. Lumumba declares Kasa-Vubu deposed; army Chief-of-Staff, Colonel Joseph Mobutu seizes power in a military coup; he decides to retain Kasa-Vubu as president.

Niger gains independence from France with Hamani Diori as president.

Mali declares full independence as the Mali Republic after the withdrawal of Senegal from the Mali Federation; President Modibo Keita establishes a one-party dictatorship.

Senegal Poet and politician, Sir Léopold Sédar Senghor, becomes Senegal's first president.

Middle East Iraq, Iran, Kuwait, Saudi Arabia and Venezuela form the Organization of Petroleum Exporting Countries (OPEC); the organization is designed to safeguard the interests of oil-producing nations.

Malaya Tuanku Syed Putra becomes head of state.

USA John F. Kennedy and Richard M. Nixon take part in the first televised debate between presidential candidates. Nixon, nursing an injured leg and sporting a 'five o'clock shadow' looks uncomfortable throughout, while Kennedy, looking relaxed, is deemed to have won.

Cuba US travellers are advised by the State Department to stay away from Cuba unless they have compelling reasons to go there. Fidel Castro nationalizes US banks in Cuba. 2,000 people cheer Castro as he arrives in New York to speak at the United Nations; clocking in at four hours 29 minutes, his speech is the longest in UN history.

••

Entertainment: The first episode of *The Flintstones* is shown on TV; it is the first animated programme to be broadcast on prime-time television.

Medicine & Health: Dr Albert Starr performs the first successful heart valve replacement in a human being; he and Lowell Edwards developed the artificial heart valve in the 1950s.

Science & Technology: Europe's first moving pavement, known as a travelator, opens at Bank Underground station in London.

Born: Colin Firth, British actor. Hugh Grant, British actor. Joan Jett, US musician (Joan Jett and the Blackhearts).

Died: Sylvia Pankhurst, suffragette, 78. Emily Post, US etiquette expert,

86. Sultan Hisamuddin Alam Shah, Sultan of Selangor, Malaya's second head of state, 62.

••

October

United Nations Soviet premier, Nikita Khrushchev embarrassingly pounds his desk with a shoe at the General Assembly in protest at a discussion of the USSR's policy towards Eastern Europe.

Algeria The OAS explodes 70 bombs in Algiers.

Nigeria gains independence from Britain; Nnamdi Azikiwe is installed as the first native governor-general.

Cameroon The formerly-British Southern Cameroons unites with the former French Cameroon to form the Federal Republic of Cameroon. Félix-Roland Moumié, Marxist leader of the banned Union des Populations du Cameroun, is assassinated in Geneva by the Service de Documentation Extérieure et de Contre-Espionnage SDECE – a French secret service agency – who poison him with thallium.

South Africa White South Africans vote to make the country a republic; the vote is carried with a majority of 74,580.

USA President Eisenhower announces an embargo on Cuba for everything apart from medical supplies and certain food products. Dr Martin Luther King is arrested during a civil rights protest in Atlanta; he is sentenced to four months in jail.

Cuba Castro introduces the Urban Reform Act, cutting rents by 50 per cent. Opponents of Fidel Castro are executed. Castro nationalizes all remaining US interests.

Panama Liberal Party leader, Roberto Francisco Chiari Remón, is elected president.

El Salvador A coup ousts President José María Lemus Lopez; he is replaced by a military junta.

India 4,000 die in a cyclone that strikes the coast of the Bay of Bengal; 10,000 more die in another one later this same month.

East Pakistan 6,000 die in a hurricane.

Japan Inejiro Asanuma, chairman of the Japanese Socialist Party is assassinated by seventeen-year-old Otoya Yamaguchi, an extreme rightist, at a televised rally for the forthcoming Lower-house election.

••

Entertainment: The Miracles' *Shop Around* is the first top ten record for Berry Gordy's Tamla Motown.

Medicine & Health: At Edinburgh Royal Infirmary, Michael Woodruffe performs the first successful kidney transplant.

Science & Technology: A rocket explosion at the Soviet Union's Baikonur Space Centre kills 91. The first electronic wristwatch is put on sale in New York.

Sport: Cassius Clay (later Muhammad Ali) wins his first professional fight, a six-round decision over Tunney Hunsaker, police chief of Fayetteville, West Virginia.

Born: Diego Maradonna, Argentinean footballer.

Died: Jim Packard (racing car driver) aged 29.

••

November

United Kingdom Penguin Books is found not guilty of obscenity for publishing D. H. Lawrence's novel, *Lady Chatterley's Lover*; the verdict is seen as a victory for free speech and ushers in a new era of liberalism; it becomes a massive bestseller, selling 200,000 copies on its first day of publication.

Belgium threatens to withdraw from the United Nations following criticism of its policy towards the Congo.

Czechoslovakia 117 die when two high-speed trains collide near Pardubice.

Democratic Republic of the Congo Patrice Lumumba flees Leopoldville; the United Nations announces its support of the government of Kasa-Vubu and Mobutu.

Cameroon Ahmadou Ahidjo is elected president following independence; he rules until 1982 and although dictatorial, makes his country one of the most stable in Africa.

Mauritania declares independence from France; Moktar Ould Daddah is president until 1978.

South Africa The ANC goes underground and dispenses with its constitution.

USA John F. Kennedy is elected 35th president, defeating Richard Nixon by 118,550 votes; he is the first Roman Catholic to hold the office and at 43, the youngest president; Lyndon B. Johnson becomes vice president. Serious rioting erupts in New Orleans following the integration of two all-white schools. Cubans are arriving in Florida at the rate of 1,000 a week.

13 November 1960
USA Sammy Davis Jr causes controversy and receives hate mail when he marries white Swedish actress, May Britt. Interracial marriages are still forbidden by law in 31 US states; only in 1967 will these laws be abolished by the US Supreme Court.

Central America President Eisenhower orders the US navy into the Caribbean after both Nicaragua and Guatemala accuse Fidel Castro of starting uprisings.

Ecuador Carlos Julio Arosemena Monroy is elected president.

Bolivia President Víctor Paz Estenssoro is elected for a second term; he introduces universal suffrage and carries out a sweeping land-reform, promoting rural education and nationalization of the country's largest tin-mines.

South Vietnam A military coup led by Pham Van Dong fails to bring down the government of President Ngo Dinh Diem; he agrees to free elections, but later reneges on his promise.

•••

Entertainment: *The Misfits*, the final film of both Clark Gable and Marilyn Monroe, is premiered.

Science & Technology: The first submarine carrying nuclear missiles, the USS *George*, takes to sea.

Born: Neil Gaiman, British author. John F. Kennedy Jr, son of US President John F. Kennedy. Jonathan Ross, British television presenter. Tilda Swinton, British actress. Stanley Tucci, US actor. Kim Wilde, British singer and gardener.

Died: Grand Duchess Olga Alexandrovna of Russia, sister of Tsar Nicholas II, 78. Clark Gable, US actor, 59. Dimitri Mitropoulos, Greek-US composer, 64. Mack Sennett, film director (*The Keystone Cops*) and producer, 80.

•••

December

United Nations The USSR vetoes Mauritania's application for membership.

United Kingdom The Archbishop of Canterbury and the Pope meet for the first time in 500 years. The last National Servicemen receive their call-up papers as conscription ends; from now on the armed services have to rely on recruits.

France tests its third nuclear weapon in Algeria. Pierre Lagaillarde, leader of the 1958 and 1960 uprisings in Algeria flees to Spain instead of appearing in court in Paris; he is sentenced to 10 years *in absentia*; he works with others to develop the activities of the far-right OAS and is finally arrested in October 1961.

Belgium King Baudouin marries Doña Fabiola de Mora y Aragon, daughter of the Spanish aristocrat, the Marquess of Casa Riera.

West Germany Richard Baer, commandant of Auschwitz concentration camp from 1944 to 1945, is arrested; he has been living near Hamburg as Karl Egon Neumann, a forestry worker; he refuses to testify and dies in suspicious circumstances of a heart attack while in detention.

Algeria 127 people die in riots during a visit by President de Gaulle; he is there in order to persuade European colonists to accept his plan for Algerian self-determination.

Ethiopia While he is on a visit to Brazil, Emperor Haile Selassie's bodyguards attempt unsuccessfully to install his son, Crown Prince Ahma Selassie as emperor against his will; the crown prince is absolved of any complicity in the coup.

Democratic Republic of the Congo Antoine Gizenga announces that he is prime minister. Patrice Lumumba is captured by government troops; the USSR calls a meeting of the UN Security Council to insist that he is released.

USA The Supreme Court upholds a Federal Court ruling that the state of Louisiana's segregation laws are unconstitutional. The United States announces that it will commit five atomic submarines and 80 Polaris missiles to NATO by the end of 1963. The Joint Strategic Planning Staff completes plans for the launch of more than 3,000 nuclear weapons at Communist countries in just a few hours, in the event of war. 134 die over Staten Island, New York City in a mid-air collision between a United Airlines DC-8 and a TWA Super Constellation.

Guatemala, El Salvador, Nicaragua and Honduras form the Central American Common Market.

Nepal King Mahendra announces the dismissal of the government and takes power.

Laos The government flees to Cambodia as civil war erupts in the capital, Vientiane; a right-wing government under Prince Boun Oum is installed.

South Vietnam The National Liberation Front is founded by opponents fighting the Diem government.

New Zealand Keith Holyoake of the National Party becomes prime minister; he will hold office until 1972.

••

Entertainment: The Lowe and Lerner musical *Camelot* opens on Broadway. In Britain, the first episode of TV soap *Coronation Street* is screened; intended originally as a 16-part series, it will become the world's longest-running soap.

Science & Technology: A five-ton Russian spaceship containing plants, animals and insects burns up on re-entry to the Earth's atmosphere. Navy Commander Leroy Heath and Lieutenant Larry Monroe establish a world altitude record of 27,874 m (91,450.8 ft), beating the previous record by 6.4 km (4 miles).

Born: Jean-Michel Basquiat, US artist. Kenneth Branagh, British actor and director. Daryl Hannah, US actor. Dave Peltzer, US author. Carol Vorderman, British television presenter.

Died: Two space dogs, Pchelka and Mushka, when *Sputnik-3* re-entered the Earth's atmosphere.

ANIMALS IN SPACE

Animals were originally used to test whether humans were capable of surviving spaceflight. On 19 August 1960, dogs Belka and Strelka (pictured above) went into space on board *Sputnik 5*, accompanied by 40 mice. They returned to Earth alive. Ham the Chimp was launched in a Mercury capsule on 31 January 1961. The Soviet Union launched mice, guinea pigs and frogs in the Vosk 3A flights in March 1961. France sent rats into space in October 1962. France also launched Felix the cat on 18 October 1963. The first tortoise in space was launched on 14 September 1968 by the Soviet Union. The United States launched Bonny, a macaque monkey, in 1969.

HIGHLIGHTS OF 1960

MAJOR FILMS

Á Bout de Souffle
Elmer Gantry
La Dolce Vita
Never on Sunday
Ocean's Eleven

Psycho
The Apartment
The Entertainer
The League of Gentlemen
The Magnificent Seven

Janet Leigh as Marion Crane in the famous shower scene from *Psycho*

HIT RECORDS

Apache The Shadows
Cathy's Clown The Everly Brothers
Chain Gang Sam Cooke
Georgia On My Mind Ray Charles
It's Now Or Never Elvis Presley
Itsy Bitsy Teenie Weenie Yellow Polka Dot Bikini Brian Hyland
Only The Lonely Roy Orbison
Save The Last Dance For Me The Drifters
Shakin' All Over Johnny Kidd & the Pirates
Walk, Don't Run The Ventures

BEST-SELLING BOOKS

French Provincial Cooking Elizabeth David
Green Eggs and Ham Dr. Seuss
Nexus Henry Miller
Summoned by Bells John Betjeman
The Hawk in the Rain Ted Hughes
The New American Poetry ed. Donald Hall

WE HAVE
LIFT OFF

1961

January

United Kingdom The farthing, in use since the 13th century, ceases to be legal tender. It is announced that a large Soviet spy network, known as the 'Portland Spy Ring' has been uncovered; five Russian spies are arrested.

France A referendum votes in favour of de Gaulle's policy in Algeria.

Denmark The world's longest strike ends after 33 years when barbers' assistants return to work.

Portugal A Portuguese cruise ship with 600 passengers on board, the *Santa Maria*, is hijacked in the Caribbean by Henrique Galvão, an opponent of Portuguese leader Antonio Salazar.

USSR The two US Air Force officers shot down in the RB-47 reconnaissance plane in June 1960 and held in prison in Moscow are released.

Africa The Casablanca group – Morocco, the United Arab Republic, Ghana, Guinea and Mali – announce plans for a NATO-style African organization to provide mutual defence.

Democratic Republic of the Congo Patrice Lumumba is executed by firing squad; the United States, other western governments – especially Belgium – and Joseph Mobutu are implicated in the killing, but no proof has ever emerged.

Nepal King Mahendra introduces the Panchayat system whereby political parties are abolished and the country is governed by village councils led directly by the king.

USA Speaking shortly before leaving office, President Eisenhower warns of the increasing power of what he calls the 'military-industrial complex'. A race riot breaks out at the University of Georgia. Italian sculptor Alfredo Fioravanti announces that he was part of a team that forged the Etruscan terracotta warriors on show in the Metropolitan Museum of Art since 1921.

20 January 1961
USA John F. Kennedy is inaugurated as the 35th president of the United States; in his inauguration speech he speaks the famous lines, 'Ask not what your country can do for you, but what you can do for your country'. He announces the establishment of the Peace Corps, an army of volunteers whose mission is to improve conditions in developing nations.

Cuba The United States severs diplomatic relations with Cuba after Fidel Castro announces he is a communist. The Guantanamo Bay base remains in US hands. At the National Reactor Testing Station near Idaho Falls, Idaho, an atomic reactor explodes, killing three military technicians.

Brazil Populist candidate Janio Quadros takes office as president after winning in a landslide.

El Salvador In an effort to stop what they describe as 'leftist excesses', a junta of two soldiers and four civilians ousts the ruling party that has been in power for only a few months.

Uruguay Eduardo Víctor Haedo succeeds Benito Nardone as president.

• •

Entertainment: The Supremes sign with Motown Records. Bob Dylan hitchhikes to New York to visit folk-singer and composer, Woody Guthrie in hospital.

Medicine & Health: A contraceptive pill, Conovid, goes on sale in British chemists.

Science & Technology: A chimp, Ham, becomes the first primate in space; he is testing the Mercury capsule that will carry American astronauts into space.

Born: Lloyd Cole, British singer-songwriter (Lloyd Cole and the Commotions). Wayne Gretzky, Canadian ice-hockey player. Todd Haynes, US film director. Natassja Kinski, German actress. Suggs (Graham McPherson), British singer (Madness).

Died: Blaise Cendrars, Swiss writer, 74. Percy Grainger, Australian composer, 79. Dashiel Hammett, novelist, 66. Erwin Schrödinger, Austrian physicist, inventor of the Schrödinger's Cat experiment and Nobel Laureate, 74.

• •

February

Europe Paul-Henri Spaak resigns as secretary general of NATO; he is succeeded by Dutch politician, Dirk Stikker.

United Kingdom 89-year-old philosopher Bertrand Russell leads a march and sit-down protest of 20,000 anti-nuclear protestors outside the British Ministry of Defence; he is arrested and jailed for seven days. The first London minicabs are introduced.

Belgium 73 people, including the entire United States figure skating team, are killed when a Boeing 707 crashes near Brussels.

Portugal The hijackers of the cruise ship the *Santa Maria* allow the crew and passengers to disembark in Brazil; Henrique Galvão and his accomplices are given political asylum.

Morocco On the death of King Mohammed V, his son, King Hassan II, 17th king of the Alawite dynasty, ascends the throne and becomes head of government.

Angola Portugal concludes peace terms with each of the three guerrilla groups seeking independence – the MPLA, FNLA and UNITA; the Portuguese Colonial War breaks out as they turn on each other, vying for control of the capital, Luanda, and international recognition.

Democratic Republic of Congo President Joseph Kasa-Vubu appoints Joseph Iléo as prime minister. It is falsely announced by the authorities that Patrice Lumumba has been killed by villagers.

South Africa withdraws from the British Commonwealth. Nelson Mandela is acquitted of a treason charge after a trial lasting four years.

USA The first volunteers in President Kennedy's Peace Corps are sent to Ghana. New Secretary of State, Dean Rusk, announces that the United States will cooperate with other American states to end tyranny whether that tyranny is of the Left or the Right.

China launches its first nuclear reactor. US$60 million of grain is purchased from Canada.

Japan 72 die in the collapse of a mine.

Laos America increases military aid.

Australia Sydney's last tram runs; it is the end of the southern hemisphere's largest public tram network.

• •

Entertainment: Cellist Jacqueline du Pré makes her debut at London's Wigmore Hall. The Beatles play the Cavern Club in Liverpool for the first time; it is a lunchtime gig.

THE CAVERN CLUB

The Cavern Club in Liverpool is most probably the best known rock 'n' roll club in the world. It was opened on Wednesday 16 January 1957 by Alan Sytner, who had been inspired by the cellar club Le Caveau in Paris. The cellar that became the club was originally used as an air raid shelter during World War II. What started out as a jazz club eventually became a hang out for skiffle groups. Gradually blues bands and beat groups started to appear on a regular basis, the first beat group being Rory Storm and the Hurricanes (which included Ringo Starr as drummer). Brian Epstein was introduced to the Beatles at the Cavern Club on 9 November 1961.

Science & Technology: *Sputnik 9* takes a dog, Chernuschka, a dummy cosmonaut, mice and guinea pigs on a mission lasting one orbit. The USSR launches the spacecraft *Venera 1* to Venus. Chemical element 103, Lawrencium, is discovered in Berkeley, California by Albert Ghiorso, Torbjorn Sikkeland, Almon Larsh, and Robert M. Latimer.

Born: Andy Taylor, British musician (Duran Duran).

Died: Philibert Jacques Melotte, British astronomer, discoverer of Jupiter's 8th satellite, *Pasiphaë*, 81. King Mohammed V of Morocco, 51. Anthony de Rothschild, British philanthropist, 73.

• •

March

United Kingdom The first American Polaris submarines, carrying nuclear missiles, sail into the Holy Loch US naval base in Scotland. Black and white £5 notes cease to be legal tender.

Rumania Gheorghe Gheorghiu-Dej becomes president; as leader of the Communist Party he has already been in power for 13 years.

USSR 145 die when a dam on the Dnieper River bursts.

Algeria A ceasefire is declared in the Algerian War of Independence.

Uganda holds its first elections; Benedicto Kiwanuka of the Democratic Party becomes the first chief minister.

Angola The United States votes against Portuguese policy towards Angola in the United Nations Security Council; leader of the National Front for the Liberation of Angola (FNLA) Holden Roberto, launches an incursion into Angola with 5,000 militants; his troops take farms, government outposts and trading centres, killing everyone they encounter; at least 1,000 white people and an unknown number of natives are killed.

South Africa Prime Minister Hendrik F. Verwoerd says his government will not tolerate attempts by other members of the Commonwealth to change his country's racial policies.

USA President Kennedy initiates a US$17 billion nuclear missile programme and increases aid to Indochina. He discusses a plan for the invasion of Cuba devised during Eisenhower's presidency. Richard Alpert – later known as Baba Ram Dass – takes psilocybin as part of the Harvard Project, an informal series of experiments in psychology involving him and Dr Timothy Leary; amongst the project's founding board is *Brave New World* writer, Aldous Huxley. Experiments had begun in 1960, but other professors at Harvard begin to raise concerns about the legitimacy and safety of the experiments.

Grenada George Clyne is elected prime minister.

. . . .

Science & Technology: Max Conrad circles the Earth in a Piper Aztec plane, in the record time of eight days, 18 hours and 49 minutes.

Born: William Hague, British politician. Ellery Hanley, British rugby league player and coach. Lothar Matthäus, German footballer.

Died: Sir Thomas Beecham, English conductor, 81. George Formby, British singer, comedian and actor, 57.

. . . .

> **❝** *A fanatic is a man who consciously over-compensates a secret doubt.* **❞**
> Aldous Huxley

. . . .

April

United Nations The General Assembly condemns South Africa for its system of apartheid.

Portugal An attempted coup fails to unseat dictator, Antonio Salazar.

Belgium Christian Democrat, Théo Lefèvre, is elected prime minister.

Algeria French paratroopers revolt led by four French generals opposed to de Gaulle's policy in Algeria; the revolt is suppressed within days.

Israel The trial of Adolf Eichmann, charged with war crimes during World War II, begins in Jerusalem; he is indicted on 15 criminal charges, including crimes against humanity, crimes against the Jewish people and membership of an outlawed organization.

Democratic Republic of the Congo The south central region of Kasai declares independence as the Federal State of South Kasai; Albert Kalonji takes power as Emperor Albert I Kalonji.

Sierra Leone is granted independence by Britain. Sir Milton Margai, a doctor who had been appointed chief minister after the Colonial Legislative Council and the Protectorate Assembly were unified in 1951 is prime minister; he is viewed as the father of the nation's independence.

Cuba 1,500 CIA-trained Cuban exiles fail to overthrow the Castro government in the disastrous Bay of Pigs invasion after President Kennedy refuses to provide air support; 200 rebels are killed and most of the remainder captured; Kennedy accepts sole responsibility; Soviet premier, Khrushchev, sends an urgent letter to Kennedy asking him to end aggression against Cuba.

Dominican Republic In the United States, exiles appeal for help against General Trujillo's dictatorship.

Belize George Cadle Price, the architect of the country's independence, becomes its first minister.

• •

Entertainment: Bob Dylan performs in New York for the first time, opening for John Lee Hooker. Judy Garland performs in her famous comeback concert at Carnegie Hall in New York.

Science & Technology: Yuri Alexeyevich Gagarin, a Russian cosmonaut, becomes the first man in space in a flight lasting 108 minutes, he orbits the Earth once in *Vostok 1* before landing safely. Robert Noye patents the integrated circuit.

Born: Jane Leeves, British actress. Eddie Murphy, US actor.

Died: Vanessa Bell, British artist, interior designer and member of the Bloomsbury group, 82. Former King Zog of Albania, in exile in France, 65.

• •

May

United Kingdom MI6 agent George Blake is exposed as a Soviet spy by Polish defector Michael Goleniewski and is sentenced to 42 years in prison for spying for the Soviet Union; he has been an agent for MI6 since 1948 and began spying for the Russians during the Korean War. Michael Ramsey, Archbishop of York, replaces Geoffrey Fisher as Archbishop of Canterbury. Betting shops open following the passing of the Betting and Gaming Act.

France Two of the four generals who rebelled in Algeria, Maurice Challe and André Zelerr, are sentenced to 15 years imprisonment; they will be freed in 1966 and pardoned by President de Gaulle in 1968.

USSR Capital punishment is extended to include economic crime.

South Africa leaves the Commonwealth and becomes an independent republic; Charles Robberts Swart, governor general, becomes the first state president.

USA The civil rights activists known as 'Freedom Riders' leave Washington DC for New Orleans to challenge racial segregation on buses and in bus terminals; a bus carrying the first group is bombed and set on fire in Alabama. At Anniston, Ku Klux Klan members have been given permission to attack these activists without fear of arrest; martial law is declared in Montgomery, Alabama as race riots break out. 27 Freedom Riders are arrested in Jackson, Mississippi; they spread their efforts to train stations and airports; Mississippi's jails become crowded.

Dominican Republic Latin America's second-longest dictatorship ends when Rafael Leonidas Trujillo Molina is shot to death in an ambush by members of his private army while waiting to meet one of his mistresses; his family have held power for around 30 years; his tyrannical administration is remembered as one of the bloodiest of the 20th century; Vice President Joaquin Balaguer is nominally in charge, but real power lies in the hands of the army.

1 May 1961
Cuba President Fidel Castro announces that he is a Marxist-Leninist and Cuba is a communist country; he abolishes elections. He offers to exchange the troops kidnapped in the Bay of Pigs debacle for 500 bulldozers.

South Korea There is a bloodless military coup; Major-General Park Chung Hee seizes power; he will be credited with the industrialization of South Korea but criticized for his authoritarian methods.

Vietnam President Kennedy authorizes the use of American advisers to aid South Vietnam against the threat from North Vietnam.

Entertainment: The revue, *Beyond the Fringe*, starring Peter Cook, Dudley Moore, Alan Bennett and Jonathan Miller, premieres in London; a favourable review by critic Kenneth Tynan helps to turn it into a comedy sensation. 18-year-old Jimi Hendrix is arrested for being in a stolen car; he is given the choice of going to jail or enlisting in the armed forces; he enlists. Harper Lee receives the Pulitzer Prize for *To Kill a Mockingbird*.

Science & Technology: Navy commander, Alan Bartlett Shepherd Jr, becomes the first American in space when he makes a 15-minute suborbital flight in a Mercury capsule; in a speech to the US Congress, President Kennedy asks Americans to work towards putting a man on the Moon by the end of the decade. German biochemist J. Heinrich Matthaei becomes the first person to recognize and understand the genetic code; it marks the birth of modern genetics; controversially, he will never win a Nobel Prize. US spacecraft *Venera 1* becomes the first man-made object to fly past the planet; unfortunately, it had lost contact with Earth a month previously and no data is returned.

Sport: Tottenham Hotspur, managed by Bill Nicholson, becomes the first English team in the 20th century to win the Football League and FA Cup double. In Scotland, manager Jock Stein moulds unfancied Dunfermline Athletic into a powerful side; they win the Scottish Cup.

Born: George Clooney, US actor. Enya, Irish musician. Dennis Rodman, US basketball player. Tim Roth, British actor.

Died: Gary Cooper, US actor, 60. Maurice Merleau-Ponty, French phenomenologist, 53. Rafael Leonidas Trujillo Molina, dictator of the Dominican Republic, assassinated, 69.

June

Democratic Republic of the Congo Moise Tshombe, pro-Western former president of the breakaway Katanga province, is released due to lack of evidence that he was involved in the murder of Patrice Lumumba.

Kuwait gains complete independence when the British protectorate comes to an end; it becomes an emirate under the leadership of Emir Abdullah Al-Salim Al-Sabah.

Iraq President Abdul Karim Qasim, announces his intention to annex Kuwait claiming that it had been part of the Ottoman Empire and therefore subject to Iraqi rule; Kuwaitis vote against the plan and the government requests help; Britain threatens to send in troops.

Qatar gains independence from Britain.

South Africa Nelson Mandela demands a national constitutional convention and threatens a nationwide campaign of non-cooperation.

> **"** *If you talk to a man in a language he understands, that goes to his head. If you talk to him in his language, that goes to his heart.* **"**

Nelson Mandela

Canada The New Democratic Party is created when the Cooperative Commonwealth Federation (CCF) and the Canadian Labour Congress merge.

USA and USSR President Kennedy and Premier Khrushchev meet in Vienna; they discuss the situation in Berlin and agree to enforce a truce within their areas of influence.

Entertainment: Producers Albert Broccoli and Harry Saltzman buy the movie rights to the books of Ian Feming, creator of James Bond. Russian ballet star, Rudolf Nureyev, defects to the West at Le Bourget airport, Paris, while travelling with the Kirov Ballet.

Science & Technology: FM multiplex stereo broadcasting is heard for the first time.

Born: Boy George, British singer-songwriter. Michael J. Fox, US actor. Ricky Gervais, British actor-comedian. Greg LeMond, US cyclist. DJ. Meera Syal, British actress-comedian.

Died: Lee de Forest, Inventor of the electron tube, 87. Carl Jung, Swiss founder of modern psychiatry, 86. George S Kaufman, Pulitzer Prize-winning US playwright-director, 72. George Washington Vanderbilt III, US philanthropist.

July

United Kingdom Peter Benenson reads in the *Daily Telegraph* about two Portuguese students imprisoned for making a 'toast to freedom' while travelling on the underground in Lisbon; enraged at the injustice, he launches Amnesty International; its stated mission is 'to conduct research and generate action to prevent and end grave abuses of human rights and to demand justice for those whose rights have been violated.'

Ireland formally applies for membership of the European Economic Community; it is rejected.

France passes a law giving inhabitants of its overseas territories freedom of worship.

Spain gives women equal rights to men. In its first terrorist action, Basque separatist group ETA tries to derail a train carrying supporters of dictator General Franco.

Vatican Pope John XXIII publishes his encyclical *Mater et Magistrate* on the topic of 'Christianity and Social Progress'.

East Germany announces that after it signs a peace treaty with the USSR it will assume full control over Allied land and air access to Berlin; West German chancellor, Konrad Adenauer, proclaims Western rights of access to Berlin. In the last 24 hours of the month, 1,322 people escape into West Berlin from the east.

USSR Premier Nikita Khrushchev announces a 30 per cent increase in the Soviet defence budget. The Soviet submarine *K-19* develops a reactor leak in the North Atlantic and she is unable to contact Moscow; her captain, Nikolai Vladimirovich Zateyev fears an explosion will make the USA think the USSR is making a pre-emptive nuclear strike and trigger nuclear war; the craft is rescued but 22 die. In 2006, the captain is nominated for the Nobel Peace Prize for his actions during the incident.

Israel welcomes its millionth immigrant. The *Shavit 2*, Israel's first rocket, is launched for meteorological research.

Burundi Union des Partis Populaires (UPP) leader Joseph Cimpaye leads his country to independence from Belgium as prime minister.

USA President Kennedy calls for an extra $3.25 million in defence spending and an increase in US and NATO forces. Jimmy Hoffa is elected president of the Teamsters Union. A commercial flight is hijacked to Cuba, the first of a number of such incidents.

Kuwait British troops arrive to provide support against Iraqi annexation threats.

China and North Korea sign a Treaty of Friendship, Cooperation and Mutual Assistance.

Entertainment: Charlie Brown, hero of Charles Schultz's comic-strip, *Peanuts*, flies his kite for the first time, having been trying for 11 years.

Science & Technology: Captain Virgil 'Gus' Grissom is the second American in space; on splashdown, the hatch opens accidentally and the craft sinks; it will be recovered in 1999.

Born: Diana, Princess of Wales. Laurence Fishburne, US actor. Woody Harrelson, US actor. Carl Lewis, US athlete.

Died: Louis-Ferdinand Céline, French author, 67. Ernest Hemingway, US author, 61.

August

East Germany begins the construction of the Berlin Wall; the United States, Britain and France protest.

USSR Premier Khrushchev predicts that the Soviet economy will surpass that of the USA. The USSR ends the three-year moratorium on nuclear tests.

Kenya Jomo Kenyatta, president of the opposition Kenya African National Union, returns from prison and exile.

Brazil President Janios Quadros resigns, initiating a serious political crisis that culminates in a military coup in 1964; he is replaced by Vice-President João Goulart after a 10-day crisis; Goulart launches a leftist programme marked by national reforms, closer ties to left-of-centre political groups, and conflict with more conservative sectors of society; he signs decrees expropriating oil refineries and uncultivated land owned by foreign companies.

South Africa Johannes Vorster, a former Nazi supporter, becomes minister of justice; during World War II he had opposed South Africa's involvement in the war on the side of the Allies.

USA President Kennedy warns that interference with Allied access to West Berlin will be considered an aggressive act for which the Soviet government will bear full responsibility.

Grenada Sir Eric Gairy of the Grenada United Labour Party is elected chief minister for the third time.

· ·

Science & Technology: Russian cosmonaut Gherman Titov circles the Earth 17 times in *Vostok-2*.

Born: The Edge (David Evans), British-born Irish guitarist (U2). Pete de Freitas, rock musician (Echo & the Bunnymen). Barack Obama, US President.

· ·

September

United Nations Secretary-General Dag Hammarskjöld dies in a plane crash in Northern Rhodesia as he flies to the Congo to negotiate a cease-fire. Future prime minister, Margaret Thatcher, is given her first government position when she is appointed parliamentary secretary at the Ministry of Pensions and National Insurance. Traffic wardens patrol London's streets for the first time. Annual roadworthy tests (MOT) are introduced by the Ministry of Transport.

United Kingdom 800 people are arrested during a CND (Campaign for Nuclear Disarmament march in London. Among those arrested are philospher Bertrand Russell, radical cleric John Collins, playwright John Osborne and actress Vanessa Redgrave.

West Germany President Kennedy increases the US garrison in West Berlin by 1,500.

Hungary Janos Kadar who will effectively rule the country until 1988 as leader of the Communist Party, becomes prime minister for a second time.

Turkey Despite appeals from world leaders, the new military government executes 15 members of the previous government, including former prime minister, Adnan Menderes, Turkey's first democratically elected leader, who is publicly hanged.

United Arab Republic A military coup in Syria ends the union between Egypt and Syria; Syria withdraws.

Ghana Strikes and demonstrations are staged in protest against President Kwame Nkrumah; he orders the arrest of strikers and political opponents.

Democratic Republic of the Congo Fighting breaks out between UN troops and forces of Katanga province.

Burundi The Tutsi Prince Louis Rwagasore replaces Hutu Joseph Cimpaye as prime minister.

Mauritania President Moktar Ould Daddah forms a government of national unity with the main opposition party, and in December, he will arrange for the four largest parties to merge as the Mauritanian People's Party (PPM), which becomes the sole legal party.

USA A law is passed punishing convicted hijackers with the death penalty. Black student James Meredith is refused access to his university in Mississippi. Allen Dulles, director of Central Intelligence – effectively head of the CIA – and his staff resign in the face of mounting criticism of the Bay of Pigs fiasco. The United States starts underground nuclear testing.

USA and USSR sign a Joint Statement of Agreed Principles for Disarmament Negotiations, known as the McCloy-Zorin Accords; they provide a roadmap for all future negotiations and international treaties with regard to nuclear and general disarmament under effective international control.

Dominican Republic Tanks line the streets following demonstrations.

· ·

Science & Technology: The Soviet Union ends a moratorium on atomic testing with a nuclear explosion in central Asia; in response, the USA resumes testing.

Sport: During Formula One's Italian Grand Prix at Monza, German driver Wolfgang Von Tripps, on the verge of winning the world championship, crashes his Ferrari into a stand, killing himself and 14 spectators.

Born: James Gandolfini, US actor.

Died: Marion Davies, US actress, 64. Hilda Doolittle (HD), US poet, 75. Dag Hammarskjöld, Swedish UN secretary-general, 56. Eero Saarinen, Finnish-US architect, 51.

· ·

October

United Nations Burmese civil servant U Thant is unanimously elected acting secretary-general to complete the unfinished term of the late Dag Hammarskjöld. Outer Mongolia and Mauritania become the 102nd and 103rd members, respectively.

France Under the orders of the head of the Parisian police force, Maurice Papon, around 40 Algerian demonstrators (some say as many as 200) are beaten and killed by police during demonstrations against a curfew that applies only to Algerians; many of their bodies are thrown into the Seine; the atrocity will finally be recognized by the French government in 1998.

East Germany There is a stand-off between US and Soviet troops in Berlin; Cold War tensions increase.

USSR The Soviet Party Congress adopts a new Communist Party programme replacing that of 1919; Communism is redefined as a party of the whole people rather than a dictatorship of the proletariat; the Congress approves the removal of Josef Stalin's body from Lenin's Tomb in Red Square as part of the de-Stalinization of the country; it is buried next to the the Kremlin walls. Khrushchev calls for the disengagement of armed forces in Central Europe and a ban on nuclear weapons being supplied to either East or West Germany.

Democratic Republic of the Congo An armistice begins in Katanga province. 13 Italian United Nations pilots are killed by Congolese rebels.

Rwanda Hutu, Grégoire Kayibanda, is elected president.

Burundi Prime Minister Prince Louis Rwagasore, elected just two weeks previously, is assassinated by a Greek national, Georges Kageorgis, while eating dinner at a hotel; Kageorgis is allegedly in the pay of the pro-Belgian Christian Democratic Party (PDC); inter-ethnic rivalries between the Hutu and Tutsi factions of UPRONA (Union for National Progress) flare shortly after; André Muhirwa, a Tutsi, becomes prime minister.

South Africa The National Party of Hendrik Verwoerd easily wins the general election.

Kuwait British troops leave; the Arab League takes over the protection of Kuwait against the threats from Iraq.

Tristan da Cunha A volcanic eruption leads to the entire population of the south Atlantic island being evacuated to wooden huts in the disused Pendell Army Camp in Merstham, Surrey, before moving to a more permanent site at a former Royal Air Force station in Calshot near Southampton; the islanders live mainly in a road called Tristan Close.

USA President Kennedy advises Americans to build fallout shelters in case of nuclear attack by the Soviet Union. An estimate by the Joint Chiefs of Staff claims that 40,000 US troops would be required to 'clean up the Viet Cong threat' and another 128,000 men would be needed to oppose North Vietnam's intervention. Secretary of Defence McNamara says that 'it is really now or never if we are to arrest the gains being made by the Viet Cong.' Members of the Communist Party are ordered to report to the police. New York's Museum of Modern Art hangs Henri Matisse's *Le Bateau* upside down; the mistake remains undiscovered for two months.

Belize Hurricane 'Hattie' kills 270 in the capital, Belize City; after the storm, the government moves the capital inland to Belmopan.

Dominican Republic Police use rifles, guns and waterhoses against demonstrators.

South Vietnam A state of emergency is declared after a communist attack.

New Zealand The death penalty is abolished.

••

Entertainment: Bob Dylan records his eponymous first album in one day for only US$400. The first issue of the British satirical magazine, *Private Eye*, goes on sale. The first issue of Marvel Comics' *The Fantastic Four* goes on sale; it will revolutionize the American comic-book industry.

Science & Technology: The USSR tests a hydrogen bomb known as Tsar Bomba over Novaya Zemlya off Northern Russia; with a force of 50 megatons, it is the largest-ever man-made explosion. Eugene F. Lally announces his invention of digital photography.

Sport: In baseball, New York Yankee, Roger Maris, beats Babe Ruth's 34-year-old home run record.

Born: Wynton Marsalis, US jazz trumpeter.

Died: Leonard 'Chico' Marx, US actor-comedian, one of the Marx Brothers, 74. Peter Lavrids Jensen, co-inventor of the electrodynamic loudspeaker, 75. Augustus John, British artist, 83.

••

November

United Nations adopts a ban on nuclear weapons; the United States disagrees with the ban. The USSR vetoes membership for Kuwait.

USA *Mercury-Atlas 5* is launched with Enos the chimp on board. The spacecraft orbited Earth twice and then splashed down off the coast of Puerto Rico.

West Germany Heinz Felfe, head of counter-intelligence at the Bundesnachrichtendienst (BND) and a veteran of the Nazi special forces, is arrested for being an agent of the KGB.

Greece Konstantinos Karamanlis becomes prime minister for a fourth time.

USSR Molotov, Malenkov and Kaganovich, all former close associates of Josef Stalin, are expelled from the Russian Communist Party. Stalingrad is re-named Volgograd.

Democratic Republic of the Congo 13 Italian United Nations pilots are killed by Congolese rebels.

Dominican Republic Two of the late President Trujillo's sons try to seize power; US warships carrying 4,000 marines appear off the coast; the Trujillo family flees the country.

South Vietnam The number of American advisers is increased from 1,000 to 16,000. Retired General Maxwell Taylor, sent to Vietnam to compile a report for President Kennedy, concludes that 'If Vietnam goes, it will be exceedingly difficult to hold Southeast Asia'; he recommends more US support. China warns the US against sending troops to Vietnam.

• •

Entertainment: Brian Epstein sees the Beatles perform at The Cavern Club for the first time. The Marvelettes' *Please Mr. Postman* becomes Tamla Motown's first number one record.

Born: Frank Bruno, British boxer. Nadia Comaneci, Romanian gymnast. KD Lang, Canadian singer-songwriter. Meg Ryan, US actress.

Died: James Thurber, US humorist, 66.

• •

December

Europe The Marshall Plan comes to an end after distributing more than $12 billion in post-war aid to re-build Europe.

Ireland *Teilifís Éireann* (later RTÉ), Ireland's first national television station, makes its first broadcast.

Albania The Soviet Union severs diplomatic relations.

15 December 1961
Israel Nazi war criminal, Adolf Eichmann, is found guilty of war crimes and sentenced to be hanged. He can be seen here at Teggart Fortress prior to his removal to the Jerusalem Court House.

Israel Nazi war criminal, Adolf Eichmann is found guilty of war crimes and sentenced to be hanged.

Syria Nazim al-Kudsi becomes president.

Democratic Republic of the Congo Katanga prime minister, Moise Tshombe, recognizes the Congolese constitution. The diamond-rich secessionist state of South Kasai is re-taken; Emperor Albert I Kalonji of South Kasai is captured by Congolese forces, but manages to escape.

Tanganyika gains independence from Britain; Julius Nyerere is prime minister.

South Africa The ANC militant Umkhonto we Sizwe wing, headed by Nelson Mandela, explodes bombs at power stations and government offices.

Goa The Portuguese enclave is annexed by India after 26 hours of fighting with Portuguese troops; 400 years of Portuguese rule ends.

USA Dr Martin Luther King and 700 civil rights demonstrators are arrested in Albany, Georgia.

Brazil 323 people die when a circus tent catches fire in Niteroi.

Dutch New Guinea changes its name to West Papua and introduces a new flag and anthem in preparation for full independence; Indonesia attempts to invade and there are skirmishes between Dutch and Indonesian troops before an agreement is reached.

South Vietnam A US aircraft carrying army helicopters and 400 US Army personnel arrives; the first direct American military support; it signals the start of the Vietnam War.

Philippines Diosdado Macapagal defeats the incumbent Carlos P. Garcia to become president; President Macapagal's daughter Gloria Macapagal-Arroyo will also become president of the Philippines in 2001.

Australia Robert Menzies is re-elected prime minister.

● ●

Entertainment: The Beatles sign a contract to be managed by local record store owner, Brian Epstein. The Beach Boys appear for the first time under that name; they enjoy their first hit, *Surfing* this year. Toy company Mattel launches the Ken doll, to partner the hugely successful Barbie. Williams' *Night of the Iguana* is premiered.

● ●

❝*Life is all memory, except for the one present moment that goes by you so quickly you hardly catch it going.***❞**

Tennessee Williams

● ●

Born: Ingrid Betancourt, Colombian politician. Bill Hicks, US comedian.

Died: Moss Hart, US dramatist, 57. 'Grandma' (Anna M) Moses, US painter, 101.

● ●

Highlights of 1961

MAJOR FILMS

Breakfast at Tiffany's
Greyfriars Bobby
Judgement at Nuremberg
Jules et Jim
Last Year at Marienbad

The Absent-Minded Professor
The Guns of Navarone
The Hustler
The Misfits

Audrey Hepburn as Holly Golightly in *Breakfast at Tiffany's*

HIT RECORDS

Blue Moon The Marcels
Halfway To Paradise Billy Fury
His Latest Flame Elvis Presley
Please Mr. Postman The Marvellettes
Runaway Del Shannon
Stand By Me Ben E. King
The Lion Sleeps Tonight The Tokens
The Wanderer Dion
Walkin' Back to Happiness Helen Shapiro
Will You Still Love Me Tomorrow The Shirelles

BEST-SELLING BOOKS

Catch-22 Joseph Heller
James and the Giant Peach Roald Dahl
The Prime of Miss Jean Brodie Muriel Spark
To Kill a Mockingbird Harper Lee
Thunderball Ian Fleming
The Carpetbaggers Harold Robbins

COLD WAR IN THE CARIBBEAN

1962

January

France In Paris, the Foreign Ministry is bombed by the far-right OAS.

Netherlands A total of 93 people die in the worst-ever Dutch train disaster at Harmelen.

Portugal withdraws from the United Nations General Assembly due to disagreements over Angola.

East Germany Conscription is re-introduced. Albania allies with China.

USA The *Mona Lisa* is on show in the United States for the first time, at the National Gallery of Art in Washington.

Cuba and the Soviet Union sign a trade agreement. Cuba's membership of the Organisation of American States is suspended. Pope John XXIII excommunicates Fidel Castro.

Dominican Republic Rafael Filiberto Bonnelly becomes president.

El Salvador Dr Eusebio Rodolfo Cordón Cea becomes interim president until July.

Peru 4,000 people die in avalanches on the Nevado Huascarán mountain.

Western Samoa becomes independent of New Zealand.

• •

Entertainment: The Beatles perform their famous unsuccessful audition at Decca Records. Two of the renowned high-wire act, the Flying Wallendas, are killed when their human pyramid collapses during a performance.

Science & Technology: US spacecraft *Ranger 3* is launched to send back data from the Moon; it misses by 35,405 km (22,000 miles).

Born: King Abdullah II of Jordan. Jim Carrey, Canadian actor and comedian.

26 January 1962
Died: Charles 'Lucky' Luciano, the infamous US gangster, died at the age of 64. Seen here in 1936.

February

Europe The European Space Agency is formed by 12 European countries.

United Kingdom The *Sunday Times* is the first British newspaper to publish a colour supplement. Six members of the Committee of the Campaign for Nuclear Disarmament are found guilty of breaching the Official Secrets Act.

France President de Gaulle calls for independence for Algeria.

East Germany Captured American U-2 pilot, Gary Powers, is exchanged in Berlin for Soviet spy, Rudolf Abel.

West Germany 299 people die in an explosion in a coal mine in Saarland. 300 people die in heavy storms on Germany's north coast.

Finland Urho Kekkonen is re-elected as president.

South Africa Prime Minister Hendrik Verwoerd announces that the Transkei area, a region situated in the Eastern Cape, is to be made self-governing; it is an effort to demonstrate that different races can have self-development.

USA Defector Lee Harvey Oswald, future assassin of President Kennedy, writes from Minsk to the US Embassy, asking to return to the United States; the Russians provide him and his wife, Marina, with exit visas. The first lady, Jacqueline Kennedy takes TV cameras on a tour of the White House.

Vietnam US planes spray areas of jungle with Agent Orange, a herbicide and defoliant containing the deadly chemical dioxin; it is intended to clear vegetation alongside North Vietnamese supply routes; in years to come, Vietnam veterans will appeal for compensation for the ill effects.

....

Science & Technology: Lieutenant Colonel John Glenn becomes the first American to orbit Earth. During a new moon and solar eclipse, there is an extremely rare grand conjunction of the planets. *Spacewar!*, the first computer game is invented; it is implemented on the DEC PDP-1 computer at the Massachusetts Institute of Technology.

Sport: Wilt Chamberlain scores 100 points in a single NBA basketball game.

Born: Garth Brooks, US country singer. Sheryl Crow, US singer-songwriter. Andy Fordham, British darts player. Steve Irwin, Australian conservationist and wildlife television personality. Eddie Izzard, British actor-comedian. Chuck Palahniuk, US writer. Axl Rose (William Bruce Rose Jr), US rock singer (Guns N' Roses).

Died: Eduard von Steiger, president of Switzerland, 80.

....

March

France and Algeria sign the Évian Accords ending the Algerian War; a formal cease-fire will come into effect on 19 March and there will be cooperative exchange between the two countries. The OAS continues its terrorist attacks on Algerians; the deputy leader of the OAS, Edmond Jouahaud, is arrested.

Angola Holden Roberto forms the Revolutionary Government of Angola in Exile; he appoints Jonas Savimbi, future leader of rebel anti-Communist group, UNITA (National Union for the Total Independence of Angola), as foreign minister.

USA The Joint Chiefs of Staff approve a plan to 'lure or provoke Castro, or an uncontrollable subordinate, into an overt hostile reaction against the US.' FBI director, J. Edgar Hoover, talks with President Kennedy about telephone calls between him and Judith Exner; the calls Exner made came from the home of gangster, Sam Giancana; Kennedy ends the relationship.

Uruguay Faustino Harrison becomes president.

Argentina José María Guido becomes president following the ousting of President Arturo Frondizi in a military coup; his presidency is marked by violent confrontations between rival military factions.

Burma General Ne Win comes to power after what is characterized as a bloodless military coup, but the young son of former president, Sao Shwe

Thaik, is shot dead and protests are ruthlessly suppressed; he announces on Burmese radio, 'If these disturbances were made to challenge us, I have to declare that we will fight sword with sword and spear with spear'; universities are closed for two years; he becomes head of state as chairman of the Revolutionary Council and also prime minister.

Vietnam President Diem orders bombing raids on suspected Viet Cong-controlled villages.

• •

Born: Clare Grogan (CP Grogan), British actor, singer and writer. Jon Bon Jovi (John Francis Bongiovi Jr), US rock singer (Bon Jovi). Sir Steven Redgrave, British five-times Olympic rowing champion.

• •

April

United Kingdom The Commonwealth Immigration Bill removes free immigration from the citizens of member states of the Commonwealth. James Hanratty is hanged for the A6 murders; many believe him to be innocent.

France 90 per cent vote for the Évian Accords in a referendum. Edmond Jouhaud, deputy to Raoul Salan in the Organisation de l'Armée Secrète is sentenced to death for his role in the attempted 1961 coup in Algeria; he is subsequently pardoned by de Gaulle and released from prison in 1967; OAS leader Raoul Salan is arrested in Algiers.

Belgium re-establishes diplomatic relations with the Republic of the Congo.

Uganda Milton Obote forms a coalition with the Buganda Royalist Party, Kabaka Yekka; the two parties win a parliamentary majority in the independence elections and Obote is appointed prime minister by Sir Walter Coutts, then governor-general.

India Jawaharlal Nehru is elected *de facto* prime minister.

USA resumes atmospheric nuclear testing after a three-year gap.

Cuba 1,179 Bay of Pigs invaders are convicted.

Jamaica Alexander Bustamente is elected prime minister, replacing Norman Manley.

• •

Science & Technology: The *Ranger 4* spacecraft crashes on the surface of the Moon and fails to send back data. Britain puts the *Ariel I* satellite into orbit; the *Ariel* space programme launches six satellites jointly funded by the NASA Office of Space Science Applications and the UK Science Research Council.

Born: John Hannah, British actor. Philip Schofield, British television presenter.

Died: Stuart Sutcliffe, British artist and musician (the Beatles), 21.

• •

May

United Kingdom The Northern Ireland general election results in a large majority for the Ulster Unionist Party. The new Coventry Cathedral is consecrated; it replaces the building destroyed by German bombing during World War II. London's last trolley bus runs; it travels from Wimbledon to Fulwell.

France Raoul Salan, founder of the terrorist organization, the OAS, is sentenced to life imprisonment.

Spain Future king, Prince Juan Carlos, marries Princess Sophia of Greece.

East Germany 12 East Germans escape to the West via a tunnel dug under the Berlin Wall.

Italy Antonio Segni is elected president of Italy.

Algeria An OAS bomb kills 110.

Israel War criminal Adolf Eichmann is hanged; his last words are 'Long live Germany. Long live Austria. Long live Argentina. These are the countries with which I have been most closely associated and I shall not forget them. I had to obey the rules of war and my flag. I am ready.'

USA Future assassin of President Kennedy, Lee Harvey Oswald, leaves the Soviet Union with his wife and daughter.

Japan 160 are killed when three trains collide near Tokyo. The OAS and the National Liberation Front (NLF) negotiate a real armistice.

Vietnam There are now 5,000 US troops in Vietnam. President Kennedy Orders the US 7th Fleet to Indochina after the Pathet Lao – the Laotian Communist organization – overruns most of Northern Laos.

••

Sport: The 1962 FIFA World Cup begins in Chile.

Born: Dave Gahan, British singer (Depeche Mode). Jimmy White, British snooker player.

••

June

USSR Riots in the Soviet town of Novocherkassk over shortages of meat and bread, rising costs and wage cuts, are ruthlessly suppressed by Russian tanks and troops; around 90 demonstrators are killed and more than 100 are arrested.

France 130 people die in the worst one-aircraft plane crash to date when an Air France Boeing 707 crashes on take-off at Orly Airport, Paris.

Algeria The last French Foreign Legion soldiers leave Algeria; following its signature of a truce with the rival FLA, the OAS announces it will continue to fight on behalf of French-Algerians.

South Africa The Sabotage Act allows house arrest and bans; it gives sabotage a minimum five-year prison sentence without parole and allows the government to ban people from being quoted in print; these sanctions cannot be challenged in court.

USA Frank Morris and John and Clarence Anglin escape from Alcatraz prison; although there is no conclusive evidence that they survive the attempt, they may be the only men ever to escape from 'the Rock'. Leftist organization Students for a Democratic Society drafts the Port Huron Statement which is highly critical of United States government policy on a range of issues. Lee Harvey Oswald is living in Fort Worth, Texas; he walks into the local FBI office and says, 'I heard you were looking for me?'; he is interviewed by FBI agents about his activities in the USSR.

••

66 *Alcatraz, the federal prison... is a black molar in the jawbone of the nation's prison system.* 99

Thomas E. Gaddis

••

West Indies 113 die in the third fatal crash of a Boeing 707 this year; it is Air France's second fatal air crash in 3 weeks.

Entertainment: The Beatles audition for George Martin at Parlophone/EMI Records; he signs the group but insists that drummer Pete Best be replaced.

Sport: Brazil defeat Czechoslovakia 3-1 in Chile to win the FIFA World Cup for the second time.

Died: Vita Sackville-West, English writer and landscape gardener, 70.

July

United Kingdom 750 people die when London is enveloped in a dense smog. In what is described in the British press as 'the Night of the Long Knives', Prime Minister Harold Macmillan sacks a third of the members of his Cabinet following the disastrous Orpington by-election. Fighting breaks out at a rally of Sir Oswald Mosley's right-wing Union Movement in London. The world's first passenger hovercraft service begins across the River Dee.

France re-establishes diplomatic relations with Tunisia.

Algeria gains independence from France; Ahmed Ben Bella becomes the first president.

Rwanda gains independence from Belgium. Burundi gains independence from Belgium.

India New Delhi is threatened by a huge swarm of locusts.

United States Wal-Mart opens its first store.

Puerto Rico becomes a commonwealth of the United States.

El Salvador Julio Adalberto Rivera Carballo, who led the 1961 coup, becomes president as candidate of the National Conciliation Party; he is often seen driving through the streets of the capital on a Harley Davidson motorbike.

Peru Following a presidential election in which none of the candidates obtains the margin of one-third needed to win, General Ricardo Pío Pérez Godoy seizes power in a military coup; he heads a junta, promising elections the following year.

Laos An agreement is signed by 14 nations at a second Geneva Conference guaranteeing the neutrality and independence of Laos; the agreement is subverted by both the United States and North Vietnam; fighting soon returns to Laos.

Cambodia Tou Samouth, leader of the Workers' Party of Kampuchea (WPK) is murdered by the government; Pol Pot and his allies begin to manoeuvre to control the party, edging out older members whom they considered to be pro-Vietnamese.

Entertainment: The Rolling Stones perform at the Marquee Club in London for the first time; they are billed as the 'Rollin' Stones'; the band line-up is Mick Jagger, vocals, Keith Richards and Brian Jones on guitar, Ian Stewart on piano, Dick Taylor on bass and Tony Chapman on drums. The first edition of *The Late, Late Show*, hosted by Gay Byrne airs in Ireland; it becomes the longest-running chat-show in the world.

Science & Technology: *Telstar*, the world's first commercial communications satellite is launched; shortly after it relays the first-ever transatlantic television signal. The US *Small Boy* explosion is the last atmospheric nuclear test at the Nevada test site. The *Mariner 1* spacecraft begins to behave erratically after launch and has to be destroyed.

Born: Tom Cruise, US actor. Wesley Snipes, US actor.

Died: William Faulkner, US writer, aged 65. G. M. Trevelyan, British historian, aged 86.

August

France French military air weaponry engineer, Lieutenant Colonel Jean Bastien-Thiry, narrowly fails to assassinate President de Gaulle; the Citroen DS in which the president and his wife are travelling in Paris is sprayed by machine gun fire from a group organized by Bastien-Thiry; no one is hurt; the incident features in the book and film, *The Day of the Jackal*.

Algeria joins the Arab League.

South Africa The CIA tips off security forces about the whereabouts of Nelson Mandela, who has been on the run for 17 months and is known in the press as 'the Black Pimpernel'; he is arrested and charged with leading workers in a strike and leaving the country illegally; he is sentenced to five years imprisonment but ultimately spends the next 27 years in prison before being released in February, 1990.

Cuba The Soviet Union believes that the USA intends to attack Cuba; it agrees to send arms to bolster Cuban defences.

Jamaica gains independence from Britain; Alexander Bustamante receives the instruments of independence from the Queen's representative, Princess Margaret, and becomes the first prime minister of the independent country.

Trinidad & Tobago gains independence from Britain; Eric Williams is prime minister; he will remain in office until 1981.

Colombia Conservative Guillermo León Valencia Muñóz becomes president.

Western New Guinea The Netherlands acknowledges that Western New Guinea is part of Indonesia.

....

Entertainment: The Beatles sack drummer Pete Best; Ringo Starr replaces him. John Lennon secretly marries Cynthia Powell after she becomes pregnant. Spiderman appears for the first time in the Marvel comic book *Amazing Fantasy # 15*.

4–5 August 1962
Entertainment: Screen siren Marilyn Monroe is found dead in her Hollywood house; she is thought to have committed suicide.

Science & Technology: The USA launches the *Mariner 2* spacecraft; it passes within 35,000 km (21,747 miles) of Venus, becoming the first spacecraft to conduct a successful planetary encounter.

....

September

Spain 440 drown in a flash flood in Barcelona.

Denmark Jens Otto Krag, leader of the Social Democrats, is elected prime minister.

Yemen Civil war erupts after Britain gives back Aden to Yemen and withdraws its troops.

USA Timothy Leary founds the International Foundation for Internal Freedom to promote research into LSD and to publish *The Psychedelic Review*. Rachel Carson's book, *Silent Spring*, said to have given birth to the environmental movement, is published.

Grenada Sir Eric Gairy is dismissed for corruption; Herbert Blaize is elected chief minister for the second time.

China and India skirmish on their communal border.

Singapore The people of Singapore support the Malayan Federation in a referendum.

••

Sport: Ex-convict, Sonny Liston knocks out Floyd Paterson in the first round to win the World Heavyweight Boxing Championship.

Born: Jack Dee, British comedian. Ruud Gulit, Dutch footballer. Ally McCoist, Scottish footballer, coach and television pundit.

Died: E. E. Cummings, US poet, 67. Ahmad bin Yahya, King of Yemen, 71.

••

66 *Then a strange blight crept over the area and everything began to change.* **99**

Excerpt from *Silent Spring* by Rachel Carson.

••

October

France In a referendum called by President de Gaulle, the French vote for the election of their president by universal suffrage.

West Germany The *Spiegel* Scandal, one of the country's biggest post-war scandals, begins when the magazine *Der Spiegel* is accused of treason for publishing an article, 'Bedingt Abwehrbereit' ('partly prepared for defence'), which is critical of the West German army's state of preparedness for an attack by the forces of the Eastern Bloc; mass protests and political demonstrations, the first in West Germany since the war, change the political landscape in the country.

Italy Politician and industrialist, Enrico Mattei, dies in a mysterious plane crash; La Cosa Nostra, the CIA and the Italian government will be the subject of speculation regarding his death.

Vatican Pope John XXIII convenes the Second Vatican Council; a conference of bishops assembled to discuss and settle matters of Church doctrine and practice, it is the first in the Roman Catholic Church for 92 years.

Uganda gains independence from Britain.

Southern Rhodesia The United Nations General Assembly asks Britain to suspend the enforcement of the new constitution; it is planned to come into effect on 1 November.

USA Escorted by federal marshals, James Meredith registers at the University of Mississippi; he is the first black student to do so. 'The New Realists', the first Pop Art exhibition is staged at the Sidney Janis Gallery in New York.

Timeline of the Cuban Missile Crisis:

9 October President Kennedy orders a U-2 reconnaissance flight over western Cuba. It is delayed by bad weather until the 14th.

10 October It is claimed in the US Senate that six intermediate-range ballistic missile bases are being constructed in Cuba.

14 October The U-2 makes its reconnaissance flight over western Cuba.

15 October The National Photographic Intelligence Center reviews photos taken during the U-2 flight and identifies objects at San Cristobal similar to Medium-Range Ballistic Missile components observed in the USSR. National Security Adviser McGeorge Bundy decides not to inform the president about the discovery of the missiles until the following day.

16 October On being informed about the missiles, Kennedy calls for a meeting of the Executive Committee of the National Security Council, later to become known as EX-COMM; at this meeting Kennedy and his advisors discuss possible diplomatic and military courses of action.

17 October Kennedy is in Connecticut campaigning for the Democratic Party and congressional candidate Abe Ribicoff. Robert Kennedy and Special Counsel, Theodore Sorensen, meet the president at the airport to inform him that the Joint Chiefs of Staff and especially the Air Force are strongly arguing for an air strike. After another U-2 flight on the night of the 17th, intermediate-range (IRBMs) SS-5 nuclear missiles are identified.

18 October Soviet Foreign Minister Andrei Gromyko and Kennedy meet for two hours. Gromyko assures Kennedy that Soviet aid to Cuba has been only for the 'defensive capabilities of Cuba.'

20 October Kennedy's press secretary announces that the president is cancelling the remainder of his campaign trip because of an 'upper respiratory infection'. Kennedy announces a television address for the next evening.

21 October Kennedy is told by General Maxwell Taylor that an air strike could not guarantee to destroy all Soviet missiles in Cuba. He decides on a quarantine of Cuba for the time being. Another U-2 flight that day reveals bombers and MiG fighters being rapidly assembled and cruise missile sites being built on Cuba's northern coast.

22 October Congressional leaders assemble at the White House for a meeting with Kennedy. They are shown the photographic evidence of the Soviet missile installations and express support, although many advocate stronger action. The president addresses the nation, announcing the presence of the missile sites in Cuba. US military forces go to DEFCON 3 – an above-normal preparedness to go to war – and reinforcements arrive at the US base at Guantanamo Bay.

23 October Kennedy orders six Crusader jets to fly a low level reconnaissance mission while US ships take up position along a line, 1,287 km (800 miles) from Cuba. Late in the evening, Robert Kennedy is sent to the Soviet embassy to talk with Ambassador Dobrynin. Kennedy receives a letter from Khrushchev in which the Soviet leader comments that there is a, 'serious threat to peace and security of peoples'. Kennedy decides to give Khrushchev more time and pulls the quarantine line back to 804 km (500 miles).

24 October Soviet ships en route to Cuba carrying suspicious cargo believed to be missiles, either slow down or reverse their course, apart from one. The US military goes to DEFCON 2 – the highest ever security position in American history.

25 October Kennedy sends a letter to Khrushchev blaming the Soviet Union for the crisis. EX-COMM discusses a proposal to withdraw US missiles from Turkey in exchange for the withdrawal of Soviet missiles in Cuba.

26 October The Soviet ship *Marucla* is cleared through the quarantine. Kennedy says that he believes the quarantine alone cannot force the Soviet government to remove its weapons from Cuba. Meanwhile, a CIA report states that there appears to be no halt in the building of the missile sites. Another reconnaissance flight reveals the Soviets are camouflaging the missiles. Khrushchev sends another letter to Kennedy proposing the removal of the missiles if Kennedy will publicly announce that the United States will never invade Cuba.

27 October A new letter from Khrushchev arrives, proposing the removal of Soviet missiles in Cuba in exchange for the removal of US missiles in Turkey. An American U-2 spy-plane is shot down over Cuba killing the pilot, Major Rudolf Anderson, and a U-2 accidentally strays into Soviet airspace near Alaska where it is intercepted by Soviet fighters. Dobrynin and Robert Kennedy meet. President Kennedy writes to Khrushchev stating that he will make a statement that the United States will not invade Cuba if Khrushchev removes the missiles.

28 October Khrushchev announces over Radio Moscow that he has agreed to remove the missiles from Cuba much to the infuriation of Fidel Castro.

In the next few weeks, both superpowers began fulfilling their promises and the crisis was over by late November. The Cuban Missile Crisis marked the climax of an acutely antagonistic period in US–Soviet relations.

• •

China and India The Sino-Indian conflict widens to include the region of Aksai Chin; China regards it as a vital strategic link and has built the National Highway Route G219 through it.

Laos Following the Geneva Agreement, US military advisors and technicians are withdrawn.

West Papua The former Dutch New Guinea comes under United Nations administration.

• •

Entertainment: The Beatles release their first single, *Love Me Do*; it reaches number 17 in the British charts. *Dr. No*, the first James Bond film, starring Sean Connery, is released in the United Kingdom.

Born: Tracey Chevalier, US author. Michael Balzary ('Flea'), Australian bassist (Red Hot Chili Peppers). Nick Hancock, British comedian and television presenter. Evander Holyfield, US boxer. Courtney Walsh, West Indian cricketer. Caron Keating, British television presenter. Tommy Lee, US musician (Mötley Crüe).

• •

November

United Nations Burmese civil servant U Thant is elected as the new secretary-general to complete the unfinished term of the late Dag Hammarskjöld.

United Kingdom agrees with France to develop the Concorde supersonic aeroplane.

France Georges Pompidou becomes prime minister.

West Germany Defence minister, Franz Josef Strauss, is sacked over his role in the *Spiegel* Scandal; he has allegedly been involved in the police action against the magazine.

Norway 21 miners die in a mining disaster at Ny-Ålesund; the government will resign in August 1963 in the aftermath of the accident.

Saudi Arabia severs diplomatic relations with Egypt following a period of unrest, for which the defection of several Saudi princes to Egypt is said to be responsible; they have renounced their titles and pledged to work for a free Saudi Arabia.

Yemen Jordan and Saudi Arabia fight on the side of the Yemeni royalist forces while Egypt fights on the republican side; the royalists claim to have killed 250 Egyptian soldiers.

India and China The Sino-Indian War ends when the Chinese capture the disputed area of Aksai Chin and unilaterally declare a ceasefire; the loss of the war brings sweeping changes to the Indian army; moves take place to ensure it is prepared for similar conflicts in future; pressure mounts on Indian prime minister Jawaharlal Nehru who is widely criticized for failing to anticipate the Chinese invasion.

South Africa The United Nations General Assembly passes a resolution condemning apartheid and calls on member states to cease military and economic relations with South Africa; sanctions are called for.

USA After defeat in the election for the governorship of California, Richard Nixon announces that he has given his last press conference and tells journalists 'you won't have Dick Nixon to kick around any more'. Andy Warhol exhibits his famous silk-screen prints of Marilyn Monroe, Coca-Cola bottles, Campbell's Soup cans and dollar bills.

ANDY WARHOL

Andy Warhol was born Andrew Warhola in Pittsburgh, Pennsylvania, in 1928. He majored in pictorial design at the Carnegie Institute of Technology and then moved to New York where he worked as a commercial artist. He also worked as an illustrator for several magazines including *Vogue*, *Harper's Bazaar* and *The New Yorker*. Warhol truly rose to fame in the 1960s, painting images from popular culture that remain icons of 20th-century art today. This work includes silk screen prints such as the Campbell's soup cans, Coca Cola bottles, dollar bills and Marilyn Monroe which are instantly recognizable today as Warhol classics. In 1968, Valerie Solanis, the founder and sole member of SCUM (Society for Cutting Up Men) walked into Warhol's studio, known as The Factory, and shot the artist. Amazingly Warhol survived the near-fatal attack. Right: *Big Torn Campbell's Soup Can (Pepper Pot)* by Andy Warhol.

Entertainment: The satirical television programme *That Was the Week That Was,* hosted by David Frost, is broadcast for the first time on British television.

Science & Technology: The term 'Personal Computer' is first used in the media.

Born: Jodie Foster, US actress. Demi Moore, US actress. Jacqui Smith, UK politician.

Died: Niels Bohr, Nobel Prize-winning Danish Physicist, 77. Eleanor Roosevelt, first lady of the United States, 78.

December

United Kingdom The 'Big Freeze' begins; the country suffers its worst snowstorms since 1881; there will be no frost-free nights until 5 March 1963. A shooting incident in London involves two men involved with call-girl Christine Keeler; when the press investigate, they discover Keeler's affairs with both British secretary of war, John Profumo, and the senior naval attaché at the Russian Embassy, Yevgeny Ivanov; the press respects Profumo's privacy.

66 *We knew we were talking about spies. I knew he knew I knew.* **99**

Christine Keeler

Monaco A revision of the principality's constitution is carried out when Prince Rainier relaxes his previously autocratic power by devolving it to advisory and legislative councils.

Vatican The first period of the Second Vatican Council comes to an end.

Democratic Republic of the Congo United Nations troops move into the last rebel positions; Moise Tshombe flees to Southern Rhodesia.

Tanganyika becomes a republic within the Commonwealth; Julius Nyerere, founder of the Tanganyikan African National Union (TANU) is the first president.

Nyasaland Britain acknowledges the right of Nyasaland (now Malawi) to secede from the Central African Federation which consists of Southern Rhodesia and the British protectorates of Northern Rhodesia, and Nyasaland.

India Daman and Diu, formerly Portuguese-controlled, is the last foreign-occupied territory to be integrated into India.

Cuba releases 1,113 men who took part in the US Bay of Pigs invasion fiasco in exchange for $53 million of food aid.

Brunei The North Kalimantan National Army revolts; it marks the beginning of the Indonesian Confrontation, a struggle between Malaysia and Indonesia over the future of the island of Borneo that lasts from 1962 to 1966; British troops arrive from Singapore and occupy all major rebel centres.

Entertainment: Bass player, Bill Wyman, joins the Rolling Stones.

Born: Ralph Fiennes, British actor.

Died: Charles Laughton, British actor and director, 63. Queen Wilhelmina of the Netherlands, 82.

HIGHLIGHTS OF 1962

MAJOR FILMS

A Kind of Loving
Birdman of Alcatraz
Days of Wine and
    Roses
Dr. No
Lawrence of Arabia
Lolita
Mutiny on the Bounty
The Loneliness of
    the Long Distance
    Runner
The L-Shaped Room
The Manchurian
    Candidate

Ursula Andress as Bond
girl Honey Ryder in *Dr. No*

HIT RECORDS

Duke Of Earl Gene Chandler
He's A Rebel The Crystals
Hey Baby Bruce Channel
I Remember You Frank Ifield
Let's Twist Again Chubby Checker
Sherry The Four Seasons
Stranger On the Shore Acker Bilk
Telstar The Tornados
The Locomotion Little Eva
The Young Ones Cliff Richard

BEST-SELLING BOOKS

A Clockwork Orange Anthony Burgess
A Day in the Life of Ivan Denisovich Alexander Solzhenitsyn
Pictures from Breughel and Other Poems William Carlos
    Williams
Silent Spring Rachel Carson
The Golden Notebook Doris Lessing
Travels with Charly: In Search of America John Steinbeck

'I HAVE
A DREAM'

1963

January

United Kingdom Labour Party leader Hugh Gaitskell dies; Harold Wilson defeats George Brown in the ballot for the party leadership. French president Charles de Gaulle vetoes Britain's application to join the EEC. The LNER Class A3 Pacific Locomotive No. 4472, *Flying Scotsman* makes its last scheduled run. The BBC withdraws its ban on the mention of sex, religion, politics and the royal family in comedy shows.

France and Germany sign the Élysée Treaty, described as a 'reconciliation treaty'.

USSR Premier Khrushchev claims that the USSR has developed a 100-megaton nuclear bomb.

Iran The Shah announces his 'White Revolution' – a six-point reform programme that calls for land reform, nationalization of the forests, the sale of state-owned enterprises to private interests, electoral changes including the enfranchisement of women, allowing non-Muslims to hold public office, profit-sharing in industry and a literacy campaign; these issues are regarded as Westernizing trends by traditionalists, especially religious scholars; Ayatollah Khomeini denounces the Shah and his programme.

Togo Sylvanus Olympio is assassinated in a military coup; Nicolas Grunitzky becomes president.

Aden is incorporated, against the wishes of much of the city's populace, as the State of Aden, and the federation is renamed the Federation of South Arabia.

USA George Wallace is elected governor of Alabama; his inauguration speech includes the words: 'In the name of the greatest people that have ever trod this earth, I draw the line in the dust and toss the gauntlet before the feet of tyranny, and I say segregation now, segregation tomorrow, segregation forever.' Harvey Gantt becomes the first black student to enter Clemson University in South Carolina, the last state to hold out against racial integration.

South Vietnam Five US helicopters are shot down in the Mekong Delta; 30 die.

· ·

Entertainment: The first discotheque, the Whiskey-a-Go-Go, opens in Los Angeles. Drummer Charlie Watts joins the Rolling Stones.

Born: Eva Cassidy, US singer. José Mourinho, Portuguese football manager. Stephen Soderbergh, US film director.

Died: Robert Frost, US poet, 88. Jean Felix Piccard, Swiss explorer, 79. Dick Powell, US actor, 59.

· ·

February

USSR offers to allow on-site inspection of nuclear testing.

Libya 500 die in an earthquake.

Iran Women get the vote.

Iraq The Arab Ba'ath Socialist Party, led by Abdul Salam Arif, seizes power in a coup; Prime Minister General Abdel Karim Qasim is executed and thousands of peasants, communists and trade unionists are murdered; the new government will remain in power for only nine months. Saddam Hussein, a junior member of the Ba'ath Party returns from exile.

USA President Kennedy announces that it is illegal for US citizens to travel to or engage in financial and commercial transactions with Cuba.

Dominican Republic Juan Bosch, a 53-year-old novelist and professor of political science, takes office as the 41st president; he is the first democratically elected president since the assassination of President Trujillo in 1961.

Cuba The United States reports that all Soviet arms have been removed from Cuba and announces it will withdraw several thousand of its 17,000 troops based in the country. Premier Khrushchev tells the USA that an attack on Cuba would lead to war.

Argentina asks Spain for the extradition of former president Juan Peron.

Japan Five Japanese cities – Moji, Kokura, Tobata, Yahata and Wakamatsu, centred around the ancient feudal city of Kokura – merge to become the city of Kitakyūshū, with a population of more than one million.

• •

Entertainment: The Beatles enjoy their first number one hit with *Please Please Me*.

Science & Technology: The first flight of a Boeing 727 takes place.

Born: Michael Jordan, US basketball player. Seal (Seal Henry Olusegun Olumide Adeola Samuel), British singer. Vijay Singh, Fijian golfer.

Died: Sylvia Plath, US poet, 30. Rajendra Prasad, first president of India, 78.

• •

March

United Kingdom The Profumo Scandal – Labour MP, George Wigg, claiming to be motivated by national security issues, gives a speech in the House of Commons in which he claims that secretary of war, John Profumo, is having an affair with call-girl Christine Keeler who is known to have been involved with a Soviet attaché; Profumo delivers a personal statement to the House in which he admits an acquaintance with Keeler, but denies there is any impropriety in their relationship. Lord Beeching issues a report on Britain's railways, calling for swingeing cuts.

March 1963
United Kingdom The divorce of the Duke and Duchess of Argyll (left) causes a sex scandal; during the marriage, the Duchess has had affairs with famous men from Douglas Fairbanks Jr to Duncan Sandys, British minister of defence; during the divorce proceedings, the Duke produces compromising Polaroid photographs of the Duchess with an unidentified man, wearing only her signature triple-string of pearls.

France Six people receive the death sentence for plotting to assassinate President de Gaulle the previous year over the Algerian crisis; de Gaulle pardons five of the plotters, but 35-year-old Lieutenant Colonel Jean Bastien-Thiry is executed by firing squad. 200,000 French miners go on strike for more money.

Algeria demands that France stops nuclear testing in the Sahara desert.

Syria The pan-Arab Ba'ath party stages a coup, pledging to restore the

United Arab Republic. President Kudsi is arrested, stripped of his civil rights as a Syrian citizen and sent into exile, with orders never to return. Luai al-Atassi becomes chairman of the National Revolutionary Command Council.

Senegal adopts a constitution.

Pakistan and China sign a historic border agreement; they agree to build the Karakoram Highway, the highest paved road in the world, from Kashgar in China to Rawalpindi in Pakistan.

USA Former British prime minister Winston Churchill is awarded honorary American citizenship. The last inmates leave Alcatraz Prison as it is closed down. Lee Harvey Oswald orders a rifle from Klein's Sporting Goods from an advert in *American Rifleman*. The last streetcar runs in Los Angeles.

ALCATRAZ

Alcatraz island received its name in 1775 when Spanish explorer Juan Manuel de Ayala charted the San Francisco Bay. He named this tiny speck of land La Isla de los Alcatraces (Island of the Pelicans), noting in his journal that it had very little to offer with its swift currents, minimal vegetation and barren ground. 72 years later, the US Army took notice of the island, seeing its possibilities as a military fortification. After several years of laborious construction, Alcatraz was established as a symbol of military strength. Because of its natural isolation, its freezing waters and dangerous currents, the US Army realized it was an ideal location for holding prisoners of war and, in 1898, the Spanish-American war boosted the population of the prison to over 450 inmates. After the catastrophic San Francisco earthquake in 1906, hundreds of civilian prisoners were transferred to Alcatraz and by the late 1920s the three-story structure was almost at full capacity. Rules were strict at Alcatraz, and any prisoners who violated these rules faced harsh disciplinary measures. Many prisoners tried to make a break for the mainland, but most never made it and usually turned back to be rescued from the freezing waters. With numerous facelifts over the years, Alcatraz became the perfect prison to house the USA's most incorrigible criminals. Famous inmates at Alcatraz included: George 'Machine Gun' Kelly, Al Capone, Henri Young, Robert Stroud (the Birdman of Alcatraz) and the longest-serving inmate Alvin Karpis (25 years, 1 month).

Guatemala Alfredo Enrique Peralta Azurdia replaces Miguel Ydígoras as president following a coup; he establishes the Institutional Democratic Party that will dominate Guatemalan politics until 1982.

Peru Junta member, General Nicolás Lindley Lopez overthrows Ricardo Pérez when he looks like reneging on his promise of free elections.

Uruguay Former schoolteacher, Daniel Fernández Crespo of the Uruguyan National Party, becomes resident.

Bali 1,900 die when Mount Agung erupts.

Cambodia American planes begin the bombing of Communist Party headquarters.

••

Entertainment: The Beatles release their first album, *Please Please Me*.

Sport: Davey Moore, US boxer, died immediately after a televized boxing match against Sugar Ramos.

Born: Elle Macpherson, Australian model. Quentin Tarantino, US film director, writer, actor.

Died: Patsy Cline, US country singer, in a plane crash, 30. William Carlos Williams, US poet, 79.

••

April

United Kingdom signs an agreement with the USA to purchase Polaris A-3 missiles. 70,000 protestors march from London to the Atomic Weapons Establishment at Aldermarston to protest about nuclear weapons.

Netherlands Victor Marijnen of the Catholic People's Party is elected prime minister.

Yugoslavia declares itself a Socialist Federal Republic; Josip Broz Tito, leader since 1943, is proclaimed dictator for life.

Jordan Palestinians demonstrate in favour of a Jordanian state on each side of the River Jordan; soldiers are mobilized and 11 people are killed.

Canada The Quebec terrorist group, the Front de Libération du Québec, bombs a Canadian army recruitment centre, killing a night watchman. Liberal Lester B. Pearson, who won the 1957 Nobel Peace Prize for his role in defusing the Suez Crisis through the United Nations, becomes prime minister, replacing John Diefenbaker and leading a minority government.

USA Dr Martin Luther King begins his first non-violent civil rights protest in Birmingham, Alabama; police use dogs and cattle prods on protestors; Dr King is arrested with others and jailed for 'parading without a permit'. New York newspapers resume publishing after a strike lasting 114 days. 129 sailors die when the US submarine *Thresher* sinks 354 km (220 miles) east of Cape Cod.

Cuba Fidel Castro visits Moscow for talks.

••

Medicine & Health: Dr James Campbell performs the first human nerve transplant.

Born: Russell T. Davis, British television producer and writer. Gary Kasparov, Russian world chess champion and political activist. Julian Lennon, British singer and son of Beatle, John Lennon. Jet Li, Chinese martial artist and actor.

••

May

Sweden Smallpox breaks out in Stockholm.

Greece Popular member of parliament, Gregoris Lambrakis, is killed when he is intentionally run over by a truck; the government is described by opponents as a moral accomplice in the murder.

USSR British businessman and MI6 operative, Greville Wynn, is convicted of spying and sentenced to eight years in prison.

Africa The Organization of African Unity (OAU) – later the African Union – is founded in Addis Ababa by Chad, Mauritania and Zambia; it immediately condemns apartheid.

Kenya Jomo Kenyatta becomes Kenya's first elected prime minister.

Pakistan A cyclone kills 22,000 in the Bay of Bengal.

USA Racially motivated bomb attacks and rioting take place in Birmingham, Alabama; thousands are arrested. University psychology professors Timothy Leary and Richard Alpert are fired from Harvard for experimenting with psychedelic drugs.

Nicaragua René Schick Gutiérrez becomes president; he is considered to be a puppet of previous president, Luis Somoza Debayle who effectively rules the country as dictator until his death in 1967.

East Indonesia Sukarno becomes president. The United Nations hands West Papua – formerly Dutch New Guinea – over to Indonesia.

South Vietnam Buddhist protests against the Diem government turn violent when troops fire into them, killing nine; Diem proclaims Buddhists to be affiliates of the communists; security is tightened around temples.

....

Entertainment: Bob Dylan releases his second album, *The Freewheelin' Bob Dylan*.

Science & Technology: The USA launches the *Telstar II* communications satellite; it makes the first transatlantic broadcast. US astronaut, Leroy Gordon Cooper completes the sixth and last mission of the *Mercury* spacecraft, orbiting Earth 22 times.

Sport: Tottenham Hotspur become the first British football club to win a European trophy when they defeat Atletico Madrid 5-1 in the final of the European Cup Winners' Cup. Ipswich Town manager, Alf Ramsey, is appointed manager of the England international football team.

Born: Mike Myers, Canadian actor and comedian. Natasha Richardson, British actress.

....

June

United Kingdom The Profumo Scandal – after intense media coverage, war minister, John Profumo, admits that he lied to the House of Commons about his friendship with call-girl Christine Keeler; he resigns from office, from the House and from the Privy Council; although it has since been shown that there was never any breach of national security, his admission rocks the Government, contributing to Harold Macmillan's illness and his resignation later in the year, as well as to the Conservative defeat by Harold Wilson's Labour Party in the 1964 general election.

France withdraws from the NATO fleet.

West Germany President Kennedy makes his famous 'Ich bin ein Berliner' speech on a visit to West Berlin.

....

> **66** *All free men, wherever they may live, are citizens of Berlin, and, therefore, as a free man, I take pride in the words: 'Ich bin ein Berliner'.* **99**

John F. Kennedy

....

Italy The Christian Democrats retain power; Giovanni Leone is elected prime minister.

Vatican Pope John XXIII dies; he is succeeded as 262nd Pope by Cardinal Giovanni Battista Enrico Antonio Maria Montini as Paul VI.

Greece Prime Minister George Karamanlis resigns following disagreements with King Paul; Panagiotis Pipinelis briefly becomes prime minister.

Israel Prime Minister David Ben-Gurion, resigns; Levi Eshkol forms the new government.

Iran Ayatollah Khomeini delivers a speech comparing the Shah to the infamous tyrant Yazid, calling the Shah a 'wretched, miserable man'; he warns him that he must change his ways or the people will be glad to see him leave the country; two days later, Khomeini is arrested and imprisoned for eight months; there are three days of rioting throughout the country in response, resulting in 400 deaths.

Burundi Hutu, Pierre Ngendandumwe, is elected prime minister.

Zanzibar is granted independence by Britain.

South Africa passes the General Law Amendment Act, suspending the right of habeas corpus; people can now be held for 90 days without any rights.

USA Governor Wallace of Alabama says he will defy an order to integrate the University of Alabama; troops are brought in to force him to allow black students Vivian Malone Jones and James Wood to enter the university; he blocks the door and then relents. President Kennedy denounces segregation as morally wrong and says it is 'time to act'. Proposing the Civil Rights Bill; Medgar Evers, field director of the NAACP in Mississippi is shot dead by a member of the Ku Klux Klan in front of his house.

South Vietnam Buddhist monk, Quang Duc, sets himself on fire in Saigon, in a protest over President Diem's government.

. . . .

Entertainment: The Rolling Stones make their first television appearance. *Cleopatra*, starring Richard Burton and Elizabeth Taylor, is one of the most expensive flops in Hollywood history.

Science & Technology: Valentina Tereshkova becomes the first woman in space on *Vostok VI*. The first home video recorder is demonstrated at the BBC in London.

Born: Johnny Depp, US actor. George Michael, British singer.

Died: John Cowper-Powys, British novelist, 91.

. . . .

July

United Kingdom British spy, Kim Philby, defects to the USSR. Myra Hindley and Ian Brady begin the series of child murders that earns them the name of 'the Moors Murderers'.

Netherlands KVP leader, Victor Marijnen, replaces Jan de Quay as Prime Minister.

Vatican The Catholic Church accepts cremation as a funeral practice.

USSR and USA sign a treaty prohibiting the testing of nuclear weapons in the atmosphere, in space or under water. They also agree to establish a communications hot line.

Yugoslavia The town of Skopje is destroyed by an earthquake; 1,800 die.

Syria Amin al-Hafez replaces Luai al-Atassi as chairman of the Presidential Council; he introduces socialist reforms and orients his country towards the Eastern Bloc.

Cuba The USA bans all financial transactions with Cuba.

Ecuador A military coup overthrows the government of President Monroy;

Admiral Ramón Castro Jijón, as head of the ruling military junta, is *de facto* ruler.

Peru Fernando Belaúnde is elected president. Economic turbulence and an increase in terrorist activities lead to human rights violations by both insurgents and the Peruvian armed forces.

••

Entertainment: Bob Dylan, Joan Baez, Phil Ochs and Pete Seeger appear at the Newport Folk Festival.

Sport: For the second time in a year, Sonny Liston knocks out Floyd Patterson in the first round to retain the Heavyweight Boxing Championship of the World.

Science & Technology: Indian engineer, Kumar Patel, invents the carbon dioxide laser; it is now widely used in industry for cutting and welding, as well as in surgery and in military range-finding, amongst other uses.

Born: Norman Cook (Fatboy Slim), British musician.

Died: Ugo Cerletti, Italian neurosurgeon, inventor of electro-convulsive therapy (ECT), 86.

••

August

8 August 1963
United Kingdom £2.6 million is stolen in the Great Train Robbery in Buckinghamshire; a number of men rob the night mail train from Glasgow to London. Ronald Biggs, perhaps the most famous of the gang, seen above at the time of his arrest, received 30 years for his part in the robbery.

Norway Following a no-confidence vote in the previous Labour government of Einar Gerhardsen after a series of mining accidents, Conservative John Lyng is elected prime minister; he remains in power for only a month.

USSR and USA The hot line is established between the USA and USSR; it will first be used during the Six-Day War between Egypt and Israel in 1967.

Republic of the Congo President Fulbert Youlou is deposed in a coup d'état and the presidency is suspended. Alphonse Massamba-Debat, Chairman of the National Council of the Revolution, is declared prime minister and the NCR becomes the only political party permitted in the country.

USA Following the march on Washington for Jobs and Freedom, Dr Martin Luther King delivers his famous 'I Have a Dream' speech in front of

250,000 people at the Lincoln Memorial in Washington. James Meredith becomes the first African-American to graduate from the University of Mississippi. Lee Harvey Oswald is arrested after fighting while handing out flyers for the Fair Play for Cuba committee; he appears in court and is fined $12. Timothy Leary, Richard Alpert, and other Harvard Project LSD researchers move to an estate in Millbrook, New York, owned by the Hitchcocks, heirs to the Mellon fortune, to continue their experiments; Leary will later say, 'We saw ourselves as anthropologists from the twenty-first century inhabiting a time module set somewhere in the dark ages of the 1960s. On this space colony we were attempting to create a new paganism and a new dedication to life as art.'

> **66** *... I have a dream that my four little children will one day live in a nation where they will not be judged by the color of their skin but by the content of their character. I have a dream today!...* **99**

Dr Martin Luther King

South Vietnam Martial law is declared. In the Xa Loi Pagoda raids, the Army of the Republic of Vietnam Special Forces vandalizes Buddhist pagodas across the country, arresting thousands and leaving hundreds dead. President Kennedy gives tacit approval for a coup against the government of President Diem.

Cambodia severs ties with Vietnam.

Science & Technology: The USA launches *Syncom 3*, the first geostationary communication satellite; it is used to telecast the 1964 Tokyo Olympics to the United States, the first broadcast across the Pacific ocean.

Born: James Hetfield, US musician (Metallica). Whitney Houston, US singer.

Died: Georges Braque, French cubist painter, 81. Guy Burgess, British defector, 52. Phil Graham, publisher of the *Washington Post*, 48.

September

United Kingdom At the Labour Party Conference in Scarborough, leader Harold Wilson makes his famous 'White Heat' speech in which he says, 'the Britain that is going to be forged in the white heat of this revolution will be no place for restrictive practices or for outdated measures on either side of industry', identifying himself as a technocrat and a reformer. Call-girl Christine Keeler is sentenced to nine months in prison for perjury. The first surviving British quintuplets are born in Aberdeen.

Italy Mafia boss, Bernardo Provenzano, is indicted for murder; he will remain on the run for 43 years.

Vatican The second period of the Second Vatican Council opens.

NINETEEN SIXTY-THREE

Norway Einar Gerhardsen's Labour Party returns to power.

Greece Stylianos Mavromichalis forms a transitional government.

Turkey The Treaty of Ankara implicitly recognizes Turkey's right to join the European Economic Community.

Chad 300 die in demonstrations in Fort-Lamy against the authoritarian rule of President François Tombalbaye.

Yemen The 35-year-old heir of the late Imam Ahmad is assassinated by the army which declares a 'free republic'.

USA In Alabama, Governor Wallace prevents the integration of Tuskegee High School by surrounding it with State Troopers; President Kennedy federalizes Alabama's National Guard to stop Governor Wallace using it to prevent integration. Four young black girls are killed in the bombing of the 11th Street Baptist Church in Birmingham, Alabama. It is announced that President Kennedy will be visiting Dallas on November 22 and 23; he will begin his 1964 re-election campaign in a state where he and Vice-President Johnson had just scraped a victory in 1960. The visit is intended to raise funds and to mediate in political infighting between Texas Democrats. After UN Ambassador, Adlai Stevenson, is jeered and jostled on a trip to Dallas, several of Kennedy's advisers caution against the visit; Kennedy refuses and Dallas police make plans for the most stringent security precautions in the city's history. Lee Harvey Oswald rents a room in Dallas, leaving his family in New Orleans.

Dominican Republic President Juan Bosch is overthrown in a coup led by Colonel Elías Wessin; he is replaced by a three-man military junta.

India Border fighting breaks out with China.

Malaysia is created when the Federation of Malaya, Singapore, North Borneo and Sarawak are merged. Indonesia refuses to recognize the new country and wages guerrilla war against it; there are race riots involving ethnic Malays and the Chinese majority.

Indonesia Indonesian president-for-life Sukarno declares that he will crush Malaysia; he claims that the new Malaysian Federation has been created to 'corner Indonesia' and that Indonesia will 'fight and destroy it'; he announces the nationalization of all British companies; in Jakarta, rioters burn down the British Embassy.

••

Sport: George Best, makes his debut for Manchester United, aged 17; he had been discovered in Belfast at the age of 15 by United scout, Bob Bishop, who immediately sent a telegram to United manager, Matt Busby, saying, 'I think I've found you a genius'.

Died: Imam Ahmad, Monarch of Yemen, 71.

••

October

United Kingdom Prime Minister Harold Macmillan resigns due to illness during the Conservative Party conference in Blackpool; Alec Douglas-Home defeats Rab Butler in a leadership election and is appointed prime minister; he renounces his peerage in order to sit in the House of Commons.

West Germany Christian Democrat Konrad Adenauer resigns as chancellor; Ludwig Erhard replaces him.

Italy A landslide into the Vaiont Dam empties the reservoir, creating a 250-metre (820 ft) high wave, which kills more than 1,450 people.

Dahomey In the country later known as Benin, a coup ousts President Hubert Maga from office.

Nigeria becomes a republic with Nnamdi Azikiwe, it's first native governor general as president.

South Africa The charges against Nelson Mandela are quashed at his trial; he is arrested immediately after, along with Walter Sisulu; they are charged with 222 acts of sabotage.

USA President Kennedy signs National Security Action Memorandum (NSAM) #263 signalling his intention to withdraw troops from Vietnam. Lee Harvey Oswald gets a seasonal job at the Texas Book Depository in Dallas, completing customer orders for books; a friend of Oswald's wife, Ruth Paine, makes a note on her calendar to say that Oswald has purchased a rifle.

Cuba and Haiti Hurricane Flora, one of the worst Atlantic storms in history, kills more than 6,000 people.

Honduras General Oswaldo López Arellano seizes power in a military coup 10 days before presidential elections are due.

Argentina The army allows elections to take place but prevents the Peronists from putting forward a candidate; Arturo Umberto Illia is elected president.

Yemen Yemeni troops and planes fight Saudi Arabian troops on Yemen's northern border.

· ·

Entertainment: The term 'Beatlemania' is coined after the Beatles appear at the London Palladium; a television audience of 15 million watches them sing *She Loves You* and *Twist and Shout*.

Born: Laura Davies, British golfer.

Died: Jean Cocteau, French surrealist poet, author, artist and film director, 73. Edith Piaf, French singer, 48.

· ·

November

East Germany allows West Berliners one day to visit relatives in East Berlin.

Vatican The Vatican Council authorizes the use of the vernacular instead of Latin in the Sacraments.

Iceland A new island is created by a volcano 8 km (5 miles) off the southern coast.

Greece George Papandreou, a lifelong enemy of the Greek monarchy, wins the election and becomes prime minister. Hundreds of people imprisoned in the communist uprising of 1944–50 are freed.

Morocco Ahmed Bahnini becomes prime minister.

Canada 118 die when a Trans-Canada Airlines flight crashes into a wooded hillside after taking-off from Dorval International Airport near Montreal.

· ·

The Assassination of President John F. Kennedy

8 November FBI Agent Winston Lawson is briefed and receives a tentative schedule of the president's Texas trip from Agent Roy H. Kellerman who is the agent in charge of arranging the timetable for trip and responsible for motorcade route. Texas governor John Connelly confirms he will be joining the president in Dallas on 22 November.

14 November Agents Lawson and Sorrels drive the route from Dallas Lovefield Airport to the Trade Mart where the president will give a speech.

15 November The motorcade route is reviewed but remains unchanged.

16 November The *Dallas Times Herald* reports that the presidential motorcade 'apparently will loop through the downtown area, probably on Main Street on its way to the Trade Mart'.

19 November A Dallas newspaper publishes the precise route of the motorcade.

7.15 Lee Harvey Oswald leaves for work at the Texas Book Depository.

8.45 President Kennedy emerges from his hotel in Fort Worth and crosses the street to greet a crowd waiting for him in a car park.

10.00 All traffic into the Dealey Plaza area is cut off by the Dallas police.

10.40
The president's motorcade leaves his hotel for Carswell Air Force Base in Fort Worth to make the flight to Dallas.

11.10 Air Force One leaves Carswell Air Force Base.

11.39 Air Force One lands at Dallas Lovefield Airport.

11.40 The presidential motorcade leaves Lovefield Airport.

12.30 President Kennedy is shot in Dealey Plaza, near the Texas School Book Depository in downtown Dallas.

12.33 Lee Harvey Oswald is confronted by Dallas police officer, Marion Baker, in the second floor lunchroom 90 seconds after the shooting; Oswald is vouched for by a supervisor; he leaves the Depository and boards a bus.

12.37 Sergeant Harkness reports he has a witness who has pinpointed the window from which the shots were fired.

12.38 President Kennedy arrives at Parkland Hospital.

12.40–45 Oswald gets off the bus and boards a taxi, telling driver William Whaley to take him to 500 North Beckley Street. A description is issued about a suspect on Dallas police radio. 'The wanted person is a slender white male about thirty, five feet ten, one sixty five, carrying what looked to be a 30.30 or some type of Winchester'. Police officer J. D. Tippit is told to go to Dallas's central Oakcliff area.

12.54 Officer Tippit arrives in the Oakland area.

1.00 The president is pronounced dead. Oswald arrives at his rooming house; he leaves after a few minutes and is seen waiting at a bus stop.

1.10 Officer Tippett's body is found shot dead in the street near the intersection of 10th St. & Patton Ave; 13 people have witnessed Oswald either shooting Officer Tippit or fleeing the scene.

1.22 A rifle is found on sixth floor of the Book Depository, first identified as a 7.5 German Mauser.

1.35 Oswald enters the Texas Theater Cinema; police arrest him at the cinema as a suspect in the shooting of Tippit.

2.04 The president's body leaves Parkland Hospital.

2.14 The president's body arrives at Lovefield Airport.

2.15 Oswald is taken into custody at the Dallas Police Department.

2.18 Kennedy's casket is placed on board Air Force One.

2.30 (approx.) J. Edgar Hoover calls Robert Kennedy to inform him that the killer is an ex-marine who defected to the Soviet Union and is also known to be a 'pro-communist nut'.

2.38 Vice-President Lyndon Baines Johnson is sworn in as the 36th President of the United States aboard Air Force One; he then orders take-off.

24 November Oswald is shot dead by nightclub owner Jack Ruby.

25 November President Kennedy is buried at Arlington National Cemetery; 90 countries are represented at his funeral.
The Warren Commission is created to investigate the assassination. Lee Harvey Oswald is buried, but the marker on his grave is stolen; it is replaced by one that reads simply 'Oswald'.

•••

Argentina declares all foreign oil contracts void.

India launches its first rocket.

Japan In twin disasters, 450 miners die in an explosion and 160 people die in a train crash.

South Vietnam Generals led by Duong Van Minh, are given secret assurances that the US will not interfere in a coup they are planning; as they carry out the coup, President Diem is offered safe exile, but chooses to escape via an underground passage to Cholon; he is taken prisoner the next day and executed with his brother in the back of an armoured personnel carrier. Diem is buried in an unmarked grave next to the US Ambassador's house; in the years following the coup, South Vietnam is unable to establish stable government; there are several coups and the North Vietnamese are able to characterize the South Vietnamese as supporters of America's colonial efforts; following the coup and assassination, many question whether the order for it was actually given by President Kennedy before he was assassinated.

Australia Robert Menzies' Labour Party wins a general election; he becomes prime minister for an eighth time.

•••

5.15: 23 November 1963
Entertainment: The first episode of *Doctor Who* is screened in the UK.

Entertainment: The Beatles *I Want to Hold Your Hand* is the first record to sell a million copies prior to release; they perform on the Royal Variety Show in front of the Queen.

Science & Technology: The US space centre, Cape Canaveral, is re-named Cape Kennedy in memory of the assassinated president. In the United States, the touch-tone telephone is introduced.

Born: Tatum O'Neal, US actor.

Died: Aldous Huxley, British author, 69. C. S. Lewis, British author, 64. Robert Stroud, (the Birdman of Alcatraz), US convict, 73.

•••

December

Portugal 128 people die when cruise liner, *Lakonia*, catches fire 289 km (180 miles) north of Madeira.

West Germany The trial of 21 Auschwitz concentration camp guards begins.

East Germany The Berlin Wall is opened briefly for Christmas.

Italy Christian Democrat, Aldo Moro, is elected prime minister; he holds power for more than five years, becoming one of Italy's longest-serving prime ministers.

Vatican The second period of the Second Vatican Council ends.

Greece Ioannis Paraskevopoulos takes over as head of a transitional government.

Cyprus The Turkish minority riot in protest at anti-Turkish changes to the constitution.

Kenya gains independence from Britain; it becomes a republic and Jomo Kenyatta is elected as its first president; he convinces rival Daniel Arap Moi that their two parties, KANU and KADU, should be merged; Kenya becomes effectively a single-party state; Kenyatta will rule for 15 years.

Republic of the Congo Prime Minister Alphonse Massamba-Debat becomes president, with Pascal Lissouba as prime minister.

Zanzibar becomes independent from Britain as a constitutional monarchy, under Sultan Jamshid bin Abdullah.

USA New York's Idlewild Airport is re-named John F. Kennedy International Airport.

Thailand Field Marshal Thanom Kittikachorn becomes prime minister, beginning a decade of military rule; his regime is marked by systemic corruption.

South Korea Park Chung-hee narrowly wins the presidential election as a candidate of the Democratic Republican Party; he remains in office until his assassination in 1979; he will be criticized for his authoritarian rule, but is also credited with the industrialization of the country through export-led growth.

•••

Entertainment: Frank Sinatra Jr, son of the singer, is kidnapped and ransomed for $240,000. Beatlemania erupts in the United States when *I Saw Her Standing There* and *I Want to Hold Your Hand* are released.

Sport: Instant replay is used for the first time on television during the Army versus Navy American football match; Army quarterback, Rollie Stichweh, is the first sportsman ever to feature.

Born: Brad Pitt, US actor.

Died: Paul Hindemith, German composer, 68. 'Gorgeous George' Wagner, US wrestler, 68. Dinah Washington, US singer, 39.

•••

HIGHLIGHTS OF 1963

MAJOR FILMS

Billy Liar

From Russia With Love

Hud

It's a Mad, Mad, Mad, Mad
World

Lord of the Flies

The Birds

The Great Escape

The Nutty Professor

The Pink Panther

The Servant

Tippi Hedren as Melanie Daniels in the Hitchcock thriller *The Birds*

HIT RECORDS

Be My Baby The Ronettes

Can't Get Used to Losin' You Andy Williams

Da Doo Ron Ron Crystals

From Me to You The Beatles

He's So Fine The Chiffons

How Do You Do It? Gerry & the Pacemakers

It's My Party Leslie Gore

She Loves You The Beatles

Up On The Roof The Drifters

Walk Like A Man The Four Seasons

BEST-SELLING BOOKS

Raise High the Roof Beam Carpenters and Seymour: An
Introduction J. D. Salinger

The Collector John Fowles

The Fire Next Time James Baldwin

The Making of the English Working Class E. P. Thompson

Trout Fishing in America Richard Brautigan

Where the Wild Things Are Maurice Sendak

BEATLEMANIA

1964

January

Vatican Pope Paul VI and Patriarch Athenagoras I meet in Jerusalem; it is the first meeting between the leaders of the Catholic and Orthodox churches since the 15th century.

January 1964
United Kingdom The first official Notting Hill Carnival is held. The concept began in 1959 in St Pancras but moves thanks to the vision of local social worker Rhaune Laslett; it becomes the second-largest street festival in the world after the Rio carnival.

France restores diplomatic relations with China.

East Germany A US training plane strays into East German airspace and is shot down by Soviet fighters; three crew members are killed.

Egypt The Palestine Liberation Organization (PLO) is created during a meeting of the Arab League; the PLO Charter is put together; it proclaims Israel to be an illegal state, pledging 'the elimination of Zionism in Palestine'.

Rhodesia and The Federation of Nyasaland is dissolved.

Northern Rhodesia Kenneth Kaunda becomes the first president of Northern Rhodesia, ending 73 years of British rule.

Zanzibar The democratically elected, predominantly Arab government of Zanzibar is overthrown by African nationalist rebels led by a Ugandan, John Okello. Sheikh Abeid Amani Karume is named president of the newly created People's Republic of Zanzibar and Pemba; several thousand Arabs and Indians are killed, thousands more detained or expelled, their property either confiscated or destroyed.

USA Senator Barry Goldwater announces his candidacy for the Republican Presidential nomination. President Jonhnson announces a 'War on Poverty'. Plans are announced to build the New York World Trade Center. Teamsters Union leader, Jimmy Hoffa, is convicted of attempted bribery of a grand juror and jailed for 15 years.

Panama During a scuffle between US students and Panamanian students trying to raise a Panamanian flag next to a US flag at a high school, the flag is torn; four days of fighting between Panamanians and US troops ensue; 22 Panamanians and four US soldiers die; President Chiari severs diplomatic relations with the USA, the first Latin American country ever to do so; negotiations begin that lead to the 1977 Torrijos-Carter Treaties that end the Canal Zone and ensure the 1999 handover of the Panama Canal to Panama.

Bahamas Sir Roland Theodore Symonette is elected prime minister for the third time.

Belize First Minister George Cadle Price becomes premier when the country achieved independence as a self-governing colony.

South Vietnam General Nguyen Khanh leads a bloodless military coup d'état; he replaces Duong Van Minh as chief of state and prime minister; Duong Van Minh is placed under house arrest but allowed to continue as a figurehead head of state.

••

Entertainment: *Meet the Beatles* is the first Beatles album to be released in the USA. *Top of the Pops* appears on British television screens for the first time.

Medicine & Health: The US Surgeon-General Luther Terry states in a report that smoking may be hazardous to the health; it is the first time that the US government has made such an announcement.

Sport: The 9th Winter Olympics open in Innsbruck in Austria.

Born: Nigel Benn, British boxer. Jeff Bezos, US founder of amazon.com. Nicholas Cage, US actor. Bridget Fonda, US actress.

Died: Alan Ladd, US actor, 50. Jack Teagarden, US jazz trombonist, 58.

••

February

United Kingdom The 18th century novel *Fanny Hill* by John Cleland, is declared obscene by a magistrate; an unexpurgated version will finally be published in 1970.

Italy The government asks the world for help in preventing the Leaning Tower of Pisa from falling over completely; a multinational taskforce of engineers, historians and mathematicians meets to discuss stabilization of the tower; a number of methods are proposed, including the addition of 800 metric tons of lead counterweights to the raised end of the base; it is found that the tilt is increasing because of softer foundations on one side.

Greece George Papandreou wins a general election and becomes prime minister once again.

Cyprus Greek and Turkish Cypriots fight in Limassol.

USA In Jackson, Mississippi, the jury trying Byron De La Beckwith for the murder of civil rights activist Medgar Evers fails to reach a verdict; he will eventually be convicted of the murder and sentenced to life imprisonment in 1994, aged 74.

Cuba cuts off the water supply to the US Guantanamo Bay naval base following the US seizure of four Cuban fishing boats off the coast of Florida.

••

Entertainment: *I Want To Hold Your Hand* becomes The Beatles first number one in America; the Fab Four arrive in the United States to riotous scenes; they are seen by 73 million Americans on the *Ed Sullivan Show* – the largest television audience in history; the British Invasion begins and British acts such as The Animals, The Dave Clark Five, Herman's Hermits and The Who enjoy great success.

Sport: Cassius Clay defeats Sonny Liston to become Heavyweight Champion of the World.

Born: Matt Dillon, US actor. Lee Evans, British comedian and actor. Sarah Palin, US politician.

••

March

Europe The European Space Research Organization – later the European Space Agency – is founded.

United Kingdom The government announces the controversial closure of 6,437 km (4,000 miles) of railway lines as recommended by Dr Richard Beeching, chairman of British Railways. Radio Caroline, Britain's first pirate radio station, begins broadcasting from just outside British territorial waters. In a clash of youth cultures, scooter-riding mods and motorbike-riding rockers fight at several seaside resorts in the south of England.

Greece On the death of his father, King Paul I, Constantine II becomes king.

USA Malcolm X, suspended from the Nation of Islam after saying that the assassination of President Kennedy was 'the pigeons coming home to roost', announces that he is founding the Black Nationalist Party. Jack Ruby is found guilty of murdering Lee Harvey Oswald; he is sentenced to death but will die of cancer before the appeal against his sentence comes to court.

Venezuela Raúl Leoni of the Acción Democrática Party, succeeds Rómulo Betancourt as president.

Uruguay Luis Giannattasio of the National Party becomes president.

Burma Head of state Ne Win issues a decree banning all other political parties, establishing a one-party state.

Sport: Cassius Clay changes his name to Muhammad Ali and joins the Nation of Islam.

CASSIUS CLAY

Cassius Marcellus Clay Jr was born on 17 January 1942, in Louisville, Kentucky and went on to become one of the world's best known heavyweight boxers. As an amateur, he won a gold medal at the 1960 summer Olympics in Rome. As a professional, he was the youngest boxer to take the heavyweight title from a reigning champion (Sonny Liston) – a record that stood until 1986. He changed his name to Muhammad Ali after joining the Nation of Islam and refused to be inducted into the US Army based on his religious beliefs. He was stripped of his boxing title and his licence was suspended for nearly four years. Ali was well known for his fighting style, which he described as 'float like a butterfly, sting like a bee'.

Born: Juliette Binoche, French actress. Prince Edward, youngest child of Queen Elizabeth II of the United Kingdom. Bret Easton Ellis, US author. Rob Lowe, US actor.

Died: Peter Lorre, US actor, 59.

April

United Kingdom The 12 men arrested for their involvement in the Great Train Robbery receive sentences totalling 307 years.

Austria Josef Klaus of the Austrian People's Party is elected chancellor.

Denmark Politically-motivated artists belonging to the Situationist movement, steal the head of the Little Mermaid statue in Copenhagen.

USSR British spy, Greville Wynne, imprisoned in Moscow since May 1963, is released in exchange for Russian spy, Gordon Lonsdale.

Burundi Tutsi Albin Nyamoya is elected prime minister.

Tanganyika and Zanzibar merge to form Tanzania.

South Africa Police arrest a number of ANC leaders including the already imprisoned Nelson Mandela on charges of sabotage – which he admits – and others, one of which, plotting a foreign invasion of South Africa, he denies. At the start of his trial, Nelson Mandela makes his famous 'I am prepared to die' speech:

❝ *During my lifetime I have dedicated myself to the struggle of the African people... I have cherished the ideal of a democratic and free society in which all persons live together in harmony ... it is an ideal for which I am prepared to die.* ❞

Nelson Mandela

India On the death of India's first Prime Minister Jawaharlal Nehru, Gulzarilal Nanda succeeds him as interim prime minister.

USA Malcolm X delivers his famous speech entitled 'The Ballot or the Bullet' in which he advises African-Americans to exercise their right to vote wisely. The New York World's Fair opens.

Panama resumes diplomatic relations with the USA.

Bhutan Modernizing Prime Minister Jigme Dorfi is shot dead by an army corporal; most of those arrested for the murder are military personnel, unhappy with his policies.

Yemen A British air attack on a fort that kills 25 people is criticized by the UN Security Council.

Brazil 21 years of military dictatorship begin when a coup, supported by the US government, ousts leftist President João Goulart; Congress elects his chief of staff, Field Marshal Humberto de Alencar Castello Branco, as president.

Laos Prince Souvanna Phouma's coalition government is overthrown by a right-wing military group; Brigadier General Kouprasith Abhay replaces him.

Entertainment: The Beatles occupy the top five positions on the American singles chart; in New York they meet Bob Dylan who introduces them to cannabis. The Rolling Stones release their first album. BBC2 begins to broadcast; *Playschool* is the first programme to be shown.

Science & Technology: IBM launches the System / 360 family of computers; it will influence computer design for years to come.

Born: Russell Crowe, Australian actor.

Died: Douglas Macarthur, US World War II general, 84.

May

United Kingdom Terence Conran opens his first Habitat store on London's Fulham Road.

Egypt Russian Premier Khrushchev performs opening of the Aswan Dam.

USA The first student protests against the Vietnam War take place across the country. The State Department announces the discovery of 40 hidden microphones in the US Embassy in Moscow.

Peru 319 die in a riot at a football match in Lima between Peru and Argentina; the trouble follows a disputed refereeing decision.

Science & Technology: At Dartmouth College in the United States, John Kemeny and Thomas Kurtz run the first computer programme written in their programming language BASIC – Beginners' All-Purpose Symbolic Instruction Code; BASIC will be included on many computers.

Born: Lenny Kravitz, US musician.

Died: Nancy Astor, Viscountess Astor, American-born British politician, 84. Jawaharlal Nehru, Prime Minister of India, 74.

June

The Vatican condemns the use of the contraceptive pill.

Cyprus Greece rejects an offer of direct talks with Turkey regarding the future of the island.

Democratic Republic of the Congo Moise Tshombe returns from exile in Spain to serve as prime minister in a new coalition government.

South Africa Nelson Mandela and seven others are convicted of charges including involvement in planning armed action, four charges of sabotage, and a conspiracy to help other countries invade South Africa; they are sentenced to life imprisonment.

USA Three civil rights workers are murdered by segregationist police officers near Philadelphia, Mississippi.

South Vietnam General William Westmoreland succeeds General Paul Harkins as commander-in-chief of US forces in Vietnam.

South Korea Following massive student demonstrations, President Park Chung-hee declares martial law.

Sport: Spain wins the European Nations Cup, beating the USSR 2-1 in the final.

Born: Kathy Burke, British actress, comedian, playwright and theatre director. Courteney Cox, US actress.

Died: Max Aitken, 1st Baron Beaverbrook, Canadian-born newspaper publisher and politician, 85.

July

United Kingdom tests a nuclear device in Nevada in the USA. Resale price maintenance, rules that prevent resellers from competing too fiercely, are abolished, leading to the rise of supermarkets.

Greece George Papandreou's Centre Union Party wins an election with a landslide victory.

USSR Anastas Ivanovich Mikoyan becomes Chairman of the Supreme Soviet.

Democratic Republic of the Congo Moise Tshombe is dismissed from his position as prime minister by President Kasa Vubu.

USA President Johnson signs the 1964 Civil Rights Act; it outlaws racial segregation in schools, public places and employment. Senator Barry Goldwater is nominated as Republican presidential candidate. Race riots last for six days in Harlem.

• •

Born: Barry Bonds, US baseball player. Sandra Bullock, US actress. Courtney Love, US musician and actress.

Died: Jim Reeves, US singer, 40.

• •

August

Europe Dirk Stikker is succeeded by Italian politician Manlio Brosio as secretary-general of NATO.

Cyprus The United Nations order a cease-fire in fighting between Greek and Turkish Cypriots.

Democratic Republic of the Congo Simba rebels capture Stanleyville, taking 1,000 westerners hostage.

Malawi Declares independence from Britain.

USA In three days of rioting in Philadelphia, stores are looted and burned, 341 are injured and more than 700 arrested. Writer Ken Kelsey and his Merry Pranksters visit Timothy Leary & Richard Alpert at Millbrook; it is a stop on their sociologically important road trip on a 'Magic Bus' with 'Further' in its destination window; Neal Cassidy, the model for the character Dean Moriarty in Jack Kerouac's novel *On the Road,* is the bus's driver.

Panama Marco Aurelio Robles Méndez becomes president.

South Vietnam Following strikes against US destroyers in the Gulf of Tonkin, planes from aircraft carriers, USS *Ticonderoga* and USS *Constellation* bomb North Vietnam; the Gulf of Tonkin Resolution is passed by Congress giving President Johnson more power to deal with North Vietnamese attacks on American troops, escalating the war. US military sources reveal casualty figures for the war; 399 have been killed, more than 1,000 injured and 17 are missing in action. South Vietnamese leader, General Nguyen Khanh, is faced with an attempted coup, rioting and demonstrations in the northern provinces, a massive labour strike in Saigon, and an armed revolt by Montagnards, the indigenous people of Vietnam's Central Highlands.

Singapore Five days of race riots erupt after Malay Muslims march in celebration of the Prophet Mohammad's birthday; marchers attack Chinese bystanders; retaliations follow against Muslims.

• •

Entertainment: Riot police are called in when trouble breaks out at a Rolling Stones performance in Scheveningen in the Netherlands. *Mary Poppins,* starring Julie Andrews, premieres in Los Angeles; it will become Walt Disney's biggest money-earner to date and will win five Academy Awards. The Supremes' *Where Did Our Love Go,* released on the Tamla Motown label, is the first of five successive number ones; they will score 12 number ones before the end of the decade.

Died: Sir Cedric Hardwicke, British actor, 71.

September

Vatican The third period of the Second Vatican Council opens.

United Kingdom The Forth Road Bridge opens. The *Daily Herald* closes after 50 years to be replaced by *The Sun*. The Biba boutique opens in London; it becomes the ultimate trendy place to be seen and to shop for anything from home furnishings to pet food.

Malta gains independence from Britain.

Mozambique FRELIMO, the Mozambique Liberation Front, initiates the Mozambican War of Independence against Portugal; it will continue until 1974 with Mozambique being granted independence in 1975.

USA The Warren Commission report into the assassination of President Kennedy is published; it states that President Kennedy was killed by Lee Harvey Oswald, acting alone; it finds that Jack Ruby similarly acted alone in killing Lee Harvey Oswald.

South Vietnam The air force of South Vietnam, under the leadership of Air Marshall Nguyen Cao Ky, crushes a coup plot against General Nguyen Khanh. Nguyen Cao Ky's political star is in the ascendancy.

Entertainment: The James Bond film *Goldfinger* opens.

Born: Keanu Reeves, US actor.

Died: Harpo Marx, US comedian, 75. Sean O'Casey, Irish writer, 84.

October

October 1964
United Kingdom
The Labour Party narrowly wins the general election, ending 13 years of Conservative Party rule. Harold Wilson becomes prime minister, replacing Sir Alec Douglas-Home, with a majority of only four seats.

France French philosopher and novelist, Jean-Paul Sartre, turns down the Nobel Prize for Literature.

East Germany 23 men and 31 women escape to West Berlin through a tunnel under the Berlin Wall.

USSR A conspiracy amongst Communist Party bosses leads to the ousting of Premier Nikita Khrushchev; he is replaced by Leonid Brezhnev as general secretary of the Communist Party and Alexei Kosygin as prime minister.

Northern Rhodesia The former British protectorate becomes the Independent Republic of Zambia.

Southern Rhodesia New British prime minister, Harold Wilson, warns Prime Minister Ian Smith against a unilateral declaration of independence.

Iraq Saddam Hussein is arrested and imprisoned for conspiring against President Arif.

USA Dr Martin Luther King becomes the youngest person to win the Nobel Peace Prize for leading non-violent resistance to end racial prejudice in the United States. The Star of India, the largest sapphire in the world, is among irreplaceable gems stolen in what is called 'the Jewel Robbery of the Century' from the American Museum of Natural History in New York City; within two days, the notorious cat burglar, smuggler, and one-time surfing champion, Jack Murphy is arrested along with two accomplices and receives a three-year prison sentence; the uninsured jewel is recovered in a locker in a Miami bus station.

Australia Serial killer Eric Edgar Cooke, nicknamed the 'Night Caller', becomes the last man to be executed in Western Australia.

• •

Sport: The Games of the 18th Olympiad start in Tokyo, Japan.

Science & Technology: The Soviet Union craft *Voskhod 1* is the first spacecraft with a multi-person crew and the first flight without space suits; the flight is cut short, landing on 13 October after 16 orbits. China becomes the world's fifth nuclear power when it explodes a nuclear device in Sinkiang. In Japan The Shinkansen high-speed rail system between Tokyo and Osaka is inaugurated; trains travel at up to 209 km/h (130 mph).

Born: Marco van Basten, Dutch footballer. Harry Hill, British comedian. Clive Owen, British actor.

Died: Pierre Cartier, French jeweller, 86. Herbert Hoover, former President of the United States, 90. Cole Porter, US composer, 73.

• •

November

Vatican The third period of the Second Vatican Council closes.

United Kingdom borrows $3 billion from foreign banks to save the pound. Parliament votes to abolish the death penalty for murder. Chancellor James Callaghan announces increases in social benefits and the introduction of capital gains tax. Britain imposes an arms embargo on South Africa.

Democratic Republic of the Congo Belgian troops capture Stanleyville, liberating around 1,600 European hostages held by rebels, but a number of the hostages die in the fighting.

USA In the presidential election, incumbent President Lyndon B. Johnson defeats Republican challenger Barry Goldwater with over 60 per cent of the popular vote. Security chiefs agree a plan for a two-stage escalation of the bombing of North Vietnam. Shortly before the presidential election, President Johnson orders the Warren Commission documents to be sealed for 75 years, to be accessible in 2039. In New York, the Verrazano Bridge, the world's longest suspension bridge, is opened to traffic.

Bolivia President Victor Paz Estenssoro is overthrown in a military coup by the head of the armed forces, General Alfred Ovando Candia.

Chile Eduardo Nicanor Frei Montalva defeats Socialist candidate Salvador Allende to replace Jorge Alessandri as president; Montalva is supported by $3 million of CIA money.

Japan Prime Minister Ikeda is diagnosed with cancer and resigns; he is succeeded by Eisaku Sato; he will serve three terms as prime minister, retaining office until 1972.

South Vietnam Five Americans die in a mortar attack at the Vien Hoa airbase.

Australia Compulsory military service is introduced because of the Indonesian Confrontation.

● ●

Entertainment: Stand-up comic, Lenny Bruce, is arrested in New York for using bad language in his act.

Born: Alistair McGowan, British comedian.

● ●

December

Italy Giuseppe Saragat follows Antonio Segni as president.

Israel The Palestinian liberation organization, Fatah, makes its first terrorist attack on Israel, launching its armed struggle for an independent Palestinian state.

Kenya becomes a republic; Jomo Kenyatta is executive president.

USA More than 800 student protestors are arrested at the University of California, Berkeley during a protest against the Vietnam War.

Mexico Gustavo Díaz Ordaz becomes president; he has an authoritarian approach to government.

Panama The United States agrees to negotiate a new Panama Canal Treaty following the violent demonstrations earlier in the year.

Cuba Che Guevara addresses the United Nations General Assembly.

CHE GUEVARA

Forty years after his death, the legend of Che Guevara remains undiminished and the Revolution equally unfinished. Ernesto (Che) Guevara was born in Rosario, Argentina, in 1928. His life changed when he witnessed the socialist government of President Jacobo Arbenz being overthrown by an American-backed military coup. Disgusted by what he saw, Guevara decided to join the Cuban revolutionary, Fidel Castro, in Mexico. In the first half of the 1960s, Guevara was the foremost figure in Latin America advocating revolution – even more so than Fidel Castro himself. By the time he was murdered in the jungles of Bolivia in October 1967, he was already a legend around the world.

Entertainment: Comedian Lenny Bruce is sentenced to four months in jail following a six-month obscenity trial. In Britain, Radio London starts broadcasting from a ship anchored off the south coast of England.

Born: Teri Hatcher, US actress.

Died: Sam Cooke, US singer 33. J. B. S. Haldane, British geneticist, 72.

● ●

Highlights of 1964

MAJOR FILMS

A Fistful of Dollars
A Hard Day's Night
Dr. Strangelove or:
  How I Learned to
  Stop Worrying and
  Love the Bomb
Goldfinger
Les Parapluies de
  Cherbourg
Marnie
Mary Poppins
My Fair Lady
It's A Wonderful Life
Zulu

Donna Reed and
James Stewart in *It's A*
Wonderful Life directed
by Frank Capra

HIT RECORDS

Baby Love The Supremes
Dancing In The Street Martha & the Vandellas
The House Of The Rising Sun The Animals
I Love You Because Jim Reeves
It's All Over Now The Rolling Stones
Leader of the Pack The Shangri-Las
My Boy Lollipop Millie
Oh, Pretty Woman Roy Orbison
She's Not There The Zombies
You Really Got Me The Kinks

BEST-SELLING BOOKS

A Moveable Feast Ernest Hemingway
My Autobiography Charlie Chaplin
Quotations from Chairman Mao Zedong (The Little Red
  Book) Mao Zedong
Naked Lunch William Burroughs
The Spy Who Came in from the Cold John le Carré
The Whitsun Weddings Philip Larkin
Understanding Media: The Extensions of Man Marshall
  McLuhan

SEX, DRUGS AND
ROCK 'N' ROLL

1965

January

United Kingdom Sir Winston Churchill dies; his funeral is watched on television by a global audience of 350 million. Gwynne Owen Evans and Peter Anthony Allen, convicted murderers, are the last men to be hanged in Britain.

Ireland The Taoiseach and the prime minister of Northern Ireland meet for the first time in 43 years.

Spain representatives of the Jewish community meet General Franco to discuss legitimizing Jewish communities in Spain; Jews had been expelled from Spain in 1492 by Queen Isabella I and King Ferdinand II.

Burundi Pierre Ngendandumwe becomes prime minister for a second time; just eight days after beginning his second term he is assassinated by a Rwandan Tutsi refugee who is employed at the American embassy in Burundi; the assassination leads to a renewed unrest between Tutsis and Hutus; Joseph Bamina becomes prime minister.

India Anti-Hindu riots break out and as a result, Hindi does not receive 'national language' status, remaining merely one of the country's 23 official languages.

USA Dr Martin Luther King begins a drive to get black people to register to vote. President Johnson outlines his vision of a 'Great Society', introducing a series of social reforms with the aim of eliminating poverty and racial injustice.

South Vietnam A military coup ousts the government led by Tran Van Huong.

Laos Two US planes are shot down while on a combat mission.
••

Entertainment: The Who release their first single *I Can't Explain*.

Sport: Sir Stanley Matthews plays his final top-flight football match at the age of 50 years and five days.

Born: Alan Cumming, British actor. James Nesbitt, British actor. Sophie, Countess of Wessex.

Died: Sir Winston Churchill, British politician, 90. T. S. Eliot, US-born British poet, 76. Alan Freed, US disc jockey, 43. Jeanette MacDonald, US actress and singer, 61.
••

February

Turkey Premier Ismet Inönü's coalition government collapses and Ali Suat Hayri Ürgüplü is asked to form a non-partisan caretaker cabinet.

Canada replaces the Union Jack with the Maple Leaf flag which has been used unofficially since 1945.

Gambia gains independence from Britain as a constitutional monarchy within the Commonwealth; a referendum on the question of replacing the monarchy in the form of British Queen Elizabeth II with a republic, fails to achieve the required two-thirds majority and Gambia remains a monarchy until 1970.

USA Former Nation of Islam leader, Malcolm X, is shot dead in front of 400 people in New York by assassins identified as former Black Muslims. Dr Martin Luther King and 770 other protestors are arrested outside the county courthouse in Selma, Alabama during a demonstration about discrimination in voting rights. Secretary of State, Robert McNamara calls for the construction of a nationwide network of nuclear bomb shelters.

Uruguay President Luis Giannattasio dies in office; Washington Beltran of the National Party becomes president.

South Vietnam Viet Cong kill eight US soldiers in a raid on a base in Pleiku; in reprisal, President Johnson orders the bombing of North Vietnam.

Science & Technology: The *Ranger 8* spacecraft sends back 7,000 photographs of the surface of the Moon.

Born: Michael Dell, US computer manufacturer. Dr. Dre, US rapper and music producer. Brandon Lee, US actor. Sophie, Princess of Monaco. Chris Rock, US actor and comedian.

Died: Nat King Cole, US singer, 49. Stan Laurel, British-born US comedian, one half of Laurel and Hardy, 74.

March

Romania Communist leader since 1948, Gheorghe Gheorghiu-Dej, dies of lung cancer; there is speculation that he has been intentionally irradiated while on a visit to Moscow because of his friendliness to the West; his protégé, Nicolae Ceausescu, becomes Communist Party leader, remaining in power until 1989; Chivu Stoica is named president.

Morocco Hundreds of people are killed by police during demonstrations for social justice in Casablanca.

Egypt Gamal Abdel Nasser is re-elected president.

Ceylon Dudley Senanayake is elected prime minister for the third time.

USA It is announced that 3,500 troops are to be sent to Vietnam, the first ground force troops from a foreign power since the war between the Vietnamese and the French; there are now almost 30,000 US troops there. Believing she has exhausted every other avenue, 82-year-old Alice Herz burns herself to death on a Detroit street in protest at the escalation of the war; the Students for a Democratic Society (SDS) organization stages the first Vietnam teach-in at the Univeristy of Michigan; 3,000 students take part. President Johnson orders 4,000 troops to protect civil rights marchers in Alabama as 200 Alabama State Troopers clash with 525 civil rights demonstrators in an incident known as 'Bloody Sunday'. Owsley Stanley starts an LSD factory in Berkeley, California, making the drug widely available for the first time; the widespread availability and cheapness (although it is often given away free) of the high quality acid made by Owsley Stanley will prove essential to the emergence of the hippie movement during the so-called Summer of Love in the Haight-Ashbury area of San Francisco in 1967.

Indonesia nationalizes all foreign oil companies.

Entertainment: Rodgers & Hammerstein's musical *The Sound of Music* premieres in New York.

March 1965
Entertainment:
Bob Dylan's album *Bringing It All Back Home* is released.

Science & Technology: Russian cosmonaut Alexsei Leonov makes the first spacewalk. America launches its first two-person space flight, *Gemini 3*. The PDP-8, produced by Digital Equipment Corporation (DEC), is the first successful commercial minicomputer.

Born: Sarah Jessica Parker, US actress.

Died: Farouk I, King of Egypt, 45.

....

April

United Kingdom The Pennine Way is opened; it stretches from Edale, in the northern Derbyshire Peak District, north through the Yorkshire Dales and the Northumberland National Park, to end at Kirk Yetholm, just inside the Scottish border.

Portugal Opposition politician Humberto Delgado and his secretary Arajaryr Moreira de Campos are found dead in a forest near Villanueva del Fresno in Spain; they are believed to have been strangled by Portuguese secret police on the orders of Portuguese dictator Salazar.

Netherlands Jo Cals of the Catholic People's Party becomes prime minister, replacing Victor Marijnen.

West Germany The West German parliament extends the statute of limitations on Nazi war crimes.

USSR Demonstrations in Yerevan demand recognition of the Armenian genocide, the systematic killing of Armenians by Ottoman Turks during and just after World War I; it is the first-ever such demonstration in the USSR.

Jordan King Hussein names his younger brother, Prince Hassan as crown prince and heir to the throne.

Democratic Republic of the Congo Che Guevara, arrives in the Congo to foment revolution; he is unsuccessful and travels to Bolivia.

India and Pakistan go to war for the second time along the West Pakistan-India frontier.

USA President Johnson authorizes the use of ground troops in combat in Vietnam. Tornadoes kill 256 in the Midwest. SDS holds its first anti-Vietnam war rally in Washington. Merry Prankster Ken Kesey is arrested for the first time for the possession of marijuana.

Cuba Che Guevara resigns his government posts and leaves the country to encourage and lead revolutionary activity in other countries.

Dominican Republic Officers and civilians loyal to the deposed president, Juan Bosch, revolt against the right-wing junta running the country; they set setting up a provisional government; when forces loyal to the deposed junta stage a counter-coup the next day, civil war breaks out; 22,800 US troops invade; the invasion is claimed to be for the protection of US citizens, the prevention of a Communist takeover and to thwart the chances of what President Johnson calls 'another Cuba'; the new government retains power.

Australia Prime Minister Robert Menzies announces that Australia will be substantially increasing the number of troops it has in Vietnam.

....

Science & Technology: The United States launches the *Intelsat 1* communications satellite, known as *Early Bird*. RC Duncan patents 'Pampers', a disposable nappy.

Sport: The first domed sports stadium, the Houston Astrodome, opens.

Born: Robert Downey Jr, US actor. Suge Knight, US record producer.

Died: Linda Darnell, US actress, 41. Edward R. Murrow, US newsreader, 57.

....

May

West Germany establishes diplomatic relations with Israel; a number of Arab nations sever relations with West Germany as a result. Former defence minister Franz Joseph Strauss is condemned in court for his behaviour during the *Spiegel* Affair.

Egypt A Pakistan International Airlines flight crashes while landing at Cairo International Airport, killing 119.

India 274 die in a mining accident in Dhanbad.

India and Pakistan engage in border fighting.

East Pakistan A cyclone kills 12,000.

USA The first draft card burnings in protest at the Vietnam War take place at University of California, Berkeley.

South Vietnam The first large-scale US Army ground forces arrive. The Viet Cong launch an offensive against the US base at Da Nang.

••

Science & Technology: The *Early Bird* satellite transmits television pictures across the Atlantic. Russian spacecraft, *Luna 5*, lands on the Moon.

Sport: Muhammad Ali defeats Sonny Liston for a second time to retain the World Heavyweight Boxing title. Scottish racing driver Jim Clarke wins the Indianapolis 500 and the Formula One Championship in the same year.

Born: Eoin Colfer, Irish author. Krist Novoselic, US musician (Nirvana). Trent Reznor, US musician (Nine-Inch Nails). Brooke Shields, US actress.

Died: Spike Jones, US composer, 53.

••

June

Hungary Gyula Kállai becomes chairman of the Council of Ministers.

Morocco King Hassan dissolves parliament and rules directly; when elections are eventually held, they are mostly rigged in favour of parties loyal to the king, causing discontent among the opposition; demonstrations and riots challenge the King's rule.

Algeria Colonel Houari Boumédienne's Revolutionary Council overthrows President Ahmed Ben Bella, Algeria's first civilian president, in a bloodless coup.

East Pakistan The second cyclone within a month kills 35,000.

Japan A mine explosion in Fukuoka kills 236.

South Vietnam President Johnson authorizes the use of US ground forces in combat. The first contingent of Australian combat troops arrives. A military government takes power; Air Marshall Nguyen Cao Ky becomes South Vietnam's youngest prime minister at the age of 34.

••

Entertainment: The Beatles are awarded the MBE by the Queen.

Science & Technology: The Big Bang Theory of the creation of the universe is supported by the announcement of the discovery of blue galaxies.

Born: Mick Doohan, Australian motorcycle racer. Bernard Hopkins, US boxer. Nigel Short, British chess grandmaster. Steve and Mark Waugh, twin Australian cricketers.

Died: Judy Holiday, US actress, 42. Freddie Mills, British boxer, 46. David O. Selznick, US film producer, 63.

••

July

United Kingdom Sir Alec Douglas-Home resigns as leader of the Conservative Party; Edward Heath replaces him. Education Secretary Anthony Crosland announces a massive expansion of comprehensive schooling in Britain; local authorities are instructed to convert schools to comprehensives. Great Train robber, Ronnie Biggs, escapes from Wandsworth prison; he will remain on the run until 2001.

France and Italy The 11.6 km- (7.2 mile)-long Mont Blanc tunnel linking the two countries is opened; drilling work began in May, 1959.

Belgium Christian Democrat, Pierre Harmel, is elected prime minister.

Greece In an incident known as the *Apostasia*, King Constantine dismisses the government of George Papandreou following a dispute over control of the Ministry of Defence.

USA President Johnson announces an increase in the number of US troops in South Vietnam from 75,000 to 125,000; he also doubles the number of men drafted per month from 17,000 to 35,000. American cigarette manufacturers are forced by law to print health warnings on cigarette packets. Ken Kesey meets fellow writer, Hunter S. Thompson who introduces the Merry Pranksters to the Hells Angels; LSD gurus Timothy Leary and Richard Alpert are at the party.

Maldives gains independence from Britain.

Science & Technology: US space probe, *Mariner 4*, sends back the first close-up images of Mars.

Entertainment: Queen Elizabeth II attends the premiere of the Beatles' film *Help*. Alf Garnett appears on British television screens for the first time when the pilot episode of *Till Death Us Do Part* is aired on BBC1.

Born: Evelyn Glennie, British percussionist. JK Rowling, British author. Saul Hudson (Slash), British-born US musician (Guns N' Roses).

Died: Wally Hammond, British cricketer, 62. Syngman Rhee, former president of South Korea, 90. Adlai Stevenson, US Democratic presidential nominee in 1952 and 1956, 65.

ROY ROGERS AND TRIGGER

On 3 July 1965, 'the smartest horse in the West' – Trigger – died at the age of 33 at the Californian ranch owned by his rider, Roy Rogers. Trigger started life as Golden Cloud and first appeared in a feature film *The Adventures of Robin Hood*, ridden by Olivia de Havilland. Roy Rogers bought Golden Cloud for $2,500 and renamed him Trigger. Roy rode his iconic palomino horse in 80 films and 100 television episodes. Trigger was so popular he had his own fan clubs all over the world. Roy did not want to bury Trigger, so instead he had his hide stretched over a plaster likeness, which is on display at the Roy Rogers Museum.

August

United Kingdom Cigarette advertising is banned on television. Elizabeth Lane, one of the first women to practice as a barrister, becomes Britain's first woman High Court judge.

West Germany The Auschwitz war crimes trials end in 66 life sentences for former members of the SS.

Switzerland 90 workers die in an avalanche at a dam construction site at Saas-Fee.

India and Pakistan India invades Pakistan without formally declaring war; fighting spreads to Kashmir and the Punjab.

Singapore leaves the Malaysian federation and becomes a sovereign nation; Lee Kuan Yew becomes prime minister.

USA The National Guard are called in during six days of rioting in the Watts district of Los Angeles; 35 die, 2,200 are arrested and an estimated $40 million of damage is caused. The burning of draft cards is made punishable by five years in prison and a $1,000 fine.

South Vietnam Operation Starlite signals the start of major US ground combat operations; the Viet Cong are routed in the Mekong Delta.

....

Entertainment: The Beatles play in front of 56,000 at New York's Shea Stadium; it is rock music's first stadium concert. Bob Dylan is booed off the stage at New York's Forest Hills when he dons an electric guitar for what some see as betrayal of his folk roots.

Science & Technology: Sony markets the CV-2000, the world's first video recorder.

Born: Dennis Lehane, US author.

Died: Le Corbusier, Swiss-French architect, 77.

....

September

United Nations Secretary General U Thant recommends China for membership.

United Kingdom BP finds oil in the North Sea.

France withdraws from NATO in protest at the American dominance of the organization. François Mitterrand is nominated as the left-wing candidate for the presidency.

Vatican The fourth and final period of the Second Vatican Council begins.

Greece King Constantine II of Greece forms a new government with Prime Minister Stephanos Stephanopoulos, in an attempt to end a two-year-old political crisis.

Tunisia President Habib Bourguiba boycotts the Congress of Arab Countries in Casablanca.

Burundi Prime Minister Joseph Bamina is assassinated.

Iraq An attempted coup by new prime minister Arif Abd ar-Razzaq ends in failure.

Aden Due to instability, the British governor cancels the constitution and takes direct control of the protectorate.

India and Pakistan Fighting continues; Indian gains followed by a Pakistani counter-attack resulting in heavy Indian losses; India gains control of two-thirds of Kashmir; the UN Security Council calls for a cease-fire; the war ends on 23 September; India has lost 3,000 troops, Pakistan 3,800.

Malaysia Sultan Ismail Nasiruddin Shah becomes head of state.

USA In an article about the Blue Unicorn Coffeehouse, San Francisco writer Michael Fallon coins the word 'hippie' to describe the new generation of beatniks who had moved from North Beach into the Haight-Ashbury district.

Cuba President Fidel Castro announces that Cubans will be permitted to emigrate to the United States.

Japan launches the world's largest oil tanker, the *Tokyo Maru*.

China announces the reinforcement of its troops on the Indian border following what it claims to be Indian provocation in the region.

South Vietnam Seven US planes are shot down in one day.

Philippines The Taal volcano erupts, killing 500.

••

Entertainment: In San Francisco, the first acid rock concert is held at Longshoreman's Hall; The Charlatans, Dan Hicks & His Hot Licks and Jefferson Airplane, in their first concert appearance, are on the bill.

Science & Technology: Japanese astronomers are the first to spot comet Ikeya-Seki.

Born: Lennox Lewis, British boxer. Moby (Richard Melville Hall), US musician. Charlie Sheen, US actor.

Died: Clara Bow, US film actress, 60. Dorothy Dandridge, US actor, 41.

••

October

United Kingdom The Post Office Tower opens; at 177 m (580 ft), it is the tallest building in Britain. 'Moors Murderers', Myra Hindley and Ian Brady are arrested.

13 October 1965
United Kingdom Model Jean Shrimpton causes a sensation when she wears a short shift dress, made by Colin Rolfe on the first day of the annual Melbourne Cup Carnival in Australia. The design, created by British designer, Mary Quant, comes to be known as the 'miniskirt'; it will be one of the defining fashions of the 1960s.

France Moroccan leftist in exile, Mehdi Ben Barka, disappears in Paris, never to be seen again.

Norway Per Borten, leader of the Centre Party, becomes prime minister.

West Germany Ludwig Erhard is elected chancellor.

Vatican Pope Paul VI visits the United States, celebrates Mass at Yankee Stadium and gives a speech to the United Nations; he issues a decree absolving Jews of collective guilt for the crucifixion of Jesus Christ.

Turkey Süleyman Demirel becomes prime minister with an unprecedented majority; he will remain in office until 1971 and will enjoy seven terms as prime minister.

Democratic Republic of the Congo President Kasa-Vubu dismisses Prime Minister Moise Tshombe and forms a provisional government.

Dahomey Military officer and political leader Christophe Soglo stages his second coup and once again takes over the government.

Burundi Prince Léopold Biha becomes prime minister following the assassination of Joseph Bamina.

Rhodesia Prime Minister Ian Smith begins negotiations with British Prime Minister Harold Wilson and Commonwealth Secretary Arthur Bottomley about Rhodesian independence; the United Nations urges Britain to try everything to prevent Rhodesia from rebelling against British rule; African countries demand that the United Kingdom uses force to prevent Rhodesia from making a unilateral declaration of independence (UDI).

South Africa At least 150 die in a train crash at Kwa-Zulu-Natal.

USA The first arrests are made for the burning of draft cards; anti-war protests draw 100,000 in 80 US cities as well as around the world.

Dominican Republic Anti-government demonstrations break out.

Brazil President Humberto de Alencar Castelo Branco withdraws power from parliament, courts and opposition parties.

Japan 209 Japanese fishermen drown when seven fishing boats are sunk in a typhoon off Guam.

Indonesia six generals are killed in an attempted coup by junior officers; the coup is ruthlessly crushed; 300,000 communists are massacred by the army and laws are passed restricting Chinese culture; the Communist Party of Indonesia is made illegal.

• •

Entertainment: Walt Disney purchases 27,000 acres in Orlando, Florida for $5 million; it will become Disney World.

Sport: The International Olympic Committee admits East Germany as a member.

Born: Steve Coogan, British writer, comedian and actor.

• •

November

United Nations The General Assembly refuses admittance to China.

France President de Gaulle announces that he will stand for re-election.

Israel Levi Eshkol is re-elected prime minister.

Democratic Republic of the Congo President Kasa-Vubu is overthrown by a military coup; Lieutenant-General Joseph-Désiré Mobutu replaces him as president; he cancels forthcoming elections and says he will rule for the next five years.

Rhodesia is put under martial law; the United Nations votes in favour of Britain using force to prevent a declaration of independence; on 11 November, Prime Minister Ian Smith, proclaims independence from Britain; the United Nations calls for a boycott.

The British Indian Ocean Territory is created; it consists of the six atolls of the Chagos Archipelago, the largest of which is Diego Garcia.

USA A massive power cut blacks out New York, several northeastern states and part of Canada for up to 13½ hours. 25,000 demonstrate against American involvement in the war in Vietnam.

Cuba 'Freedom Flights', begin between the USA and Cuba; by 1971, 250,000 Cubans will have flown to the United States.

South Vietnam A further 90,000 US troops arrive; the first major engagement between regular US troops and North Vietnamese forces begins in the La Drang Valley in the Central Highlands of Vietnam.

• •

Entertainment: Bob Dylan marries Sarah Lowndes and moves to Woodstock. The first 'acid test' psychedelic party, hosted by the Merry Pranksters is held in the San Francisco area; it is the first time a light show is used at a concert.

THE MERRY PRANKSTERS' BUS

The Merry Pranksters were a group of people who formed around the American author, Ken Kesey, most famous for his novel, *One Flew Over the Cuckoo's Nest*. They were a social, intellectual and artistic movement who promoted the use of psychedelic drugs. The group are particularly noted for their long road trip which they took in the summer of 1964. They travelled across the United States in a school bus painted in psychedelic patterns using Day-Glo colours, enigmatically labelled 'Furthur', an infusion of both 'further' and 'future'. The bus was specially adapted for the trip with the seats being replaced by couches, and intricate sound and film equipment, not just for entertainment, but to document the outing as well. The Merry Pranksters' mentor, Kesey, had first come across LSD when he was a graduate student at Stanford. Wanting to earn some extra money, he volunteered at Menlo Park VA hospital in a government-sponsored programme, participating in experiments conducted to study the effects of hallucinogens. The Acid Test Graduation in October 1966, was sponsored by the Pranksters and presided over by Ken Kesey, and held in a warehouse called the 'Rat Shack'. The aim was to get LSD to a bigger audience. However, the Graduation was a failure because Kesey could not get the acidheads on his side, and he became a scapegoat for the legal problems many of them were beginning to face.

Science & Technology: France becomes the third country into space when it launches a Diamant-A rocket with its first satellite, *Asterix-1* on board from the Hammaguira launch facility in the Sahara Desert.

2 November 1965
Sport: American Craig Breedlove sets a new land speed record of 893.666 km/h (555.485 mph) in the *Spirit of America Sonic 1*, a jet-propelled car, at Bonneville Salt Flats in Nevada. Thirteen days later, on 15 November, Breedlove breached the 965 km/h (600 mph) barrier reaching 966.961 km/h (600.842 mph) in the same car at Bonneville Salt Flats, breaking yet another record.

Born: Björk, Icelandic singer. Ben Stiller, US actor. Bryn Terfel, Welsh tenor.
Died: Dame Myra Hess, British pianist, 75.

December
United Kingdom A top speed of 127 km/h (70 mph) is imposed on British motorways.
France In the presidential election, François Mitterand gets 31.6 per cent of the vote denying the incumbent, President de Gaulle, a first-round victory; de Gaulle wins in the second round and is re-elected.
West Germany Former chancellor, Konrad Adenauer resigns as chairman of the Christian Democrat Party.
Vatican The Second Vatican Council closes.
USSR Anastas Ivanovich Mikoyan retires; Nikolai Podgorny succeeds him as chairman of the Supreme Soviet; he will hold the position until 1977.
Central African Republic Colonel Jean-Bédel Bokassa seizes power, preventing a coup by a rival, Colonel Jean Izamo, head of the national gendarme police force; President Dacko is placed under house arrest, but later becomes personal counsellor to Bokassa.
Dahomey The government changes again with a military coup.
Rhodesia The British and American governments announce an oil embargo

against Rhodesia. Organisation of African Unity members threaten to sever diplomatic relations with Britain unless it ends the Rhodesian situation by mid-December; Tanzania and Guinea do so on 15 December.

India establishes a Border Security Force to protect its frontiers.

Pakistan A cyclone kills 10,000.

USA Timothy Leary is arrested for possession of marijuana at the Mexican border.

....

66 *There are three side effects of acid: enhanced long-term memory, decreased short-term memory, and I forget the third.* 99

Timothy Leary

....

South Vietnam There are now 184,300 US troops in Vietnam; a Christmas truce is observed in the war. The USSR announces it has sent missiles to North Vietnam.

Philippines Following a campaign marked by violence and bitterness, Ferdinand Marcos is elected the country's sixth president; he will rule until he is removed from office in 1986, but his time in office is marred by massive government corruption, despotism, nepotism, political repression and human rights violations.

Tonga Taufa'ahau Tupou IV becomes king.

....

Entertainment: The Beatles begin their final UK tour in Glasgow.

Science & Technology: Two manned US spacecraft, *Gemini* 6 and 7, manoeuvre to within 3 m (10 ft) of each other while in orbit; it is the first rendezvous of manned spacecraft in orbit.

Sport: Sherman Poppen makes the first snowboard by screwing together two pairs of children's skis; he calls it the 'Snurfer'.

Born: Katarina Witt, West German figure skater.

Died: Somerset Maugham, British author, 91. Salote Tupou III, Queen of Tonga, 65.

....

HIGHLIGHTS OF 1965

MAJOR FILMS

Darling
Doctor Zhivago
For a Few Dollars More
Help!
The Ipcress File

The Knack . . . and How to Get It
The Sound of Music
The Spy Who Came in From the
    Cold
Thunderball
What's New Pussycat

Sean Connery in a love scene with Italian actress Luciana Paoluzzi
from the James Bond movie *Thunderball*.

HIT RECORDS

Help! The Beatles
I Can't Help Myself The Four Tops
I Got You (I Feel Good) James Brown
I Got You Babe Sonny & Cher
I'm Alive The Hollies
It's Not Unusual Tom Jones
King of the Road Roger Miller
Like A Rolling Stone Bob Dylan
Mr. Tambourine Man The Byrds
(I Can't Get No) Satisfaction The Rolling Stones

BEST-SELLING BOOKS

77 Dream Songs John Berryman
Ariel Sylvia Plath
Generation X Charles Hamblett and Jane Deverson
The Autobiography of Malcolm X Alex Haley
The Kandy-Kolored Tangerine-Flake Streamline Baby Tom
    Wolfe
The Sailor Who Fell From Grace with the Sea Yukio Mishima
The Looking Glass War John Le Carre

'TURN ON, TUNE IN, DROP OUT'

1966

January

Belgium In the north-eastern province of Limburg, Flemish miners demonstrate against plans for the closure of their coalmines; in the confrontation with the authorities, two miners are shot dead.

Spain A US Air Force B-52, carrying four unarmed hydrogen bombs, collides with a refuelling plane above the Spanish coast at Palomares; one of the bombs is not found until April. The first native Jewish child is born in Spain since the expulsion of the Jews from the country in 1492.

Hungary Demonstrations break out against high food prices.

Chad Civil war begins with the founding of the insurgent group FROLINAT (The National Liberation Front of Chad).

Upper Volta President Maurice Yaméogo is deposed by a military coup; Lieutenant-Colonel Sangoulé Lamizana becomes head of a government of senior army officers.

Nigeria A violent military coup deposes the government of Nnamdi Azikiwe; Major General Johnson Aguiyi-Ironsi becomes head of state; he remains in power for only 194 days.

Rhodesia Britain ceases all trade with Rhodesia.

India and Pakistan The Tashkent Agreement officially ends the 17-day war between the two countries; they agree to withdraw to positions held prior to 5 August 1965; Indian prime minister, Lal Bahadur Shastri, dies the day after signing the agreement; Indira Gandhi, daughter of Nehru, the country's first prime minister, is elected India's third prime minister, and is the first and only woman to hold the office to-date.

Brazil 550 die in landslides in mountains behind Rio de Janeiro after heavy rain.

South Vietnam US troops move into the Mekong Delta for the first time; the US Air Force resumes the bombing of North Vietnam after a 37-day pause.

Cambodia warns the United Nations that it will retaliate if United States and South Vietnamese troops fail to end intrusions.

Malaysia The British government promises that its troops will remain in the country until there is peace in the region.

Australia Liberal Party prime minister, Robert Menzies retires; Harold Holt replaces him.

. . . .

Died: Vincent Auriol, President of France 1947–54, 81. Alberto Giacometti, Swiss-French sculptor, 64.

. . . .

February

Belgium The entire government resigns during a threat of nationwide strike action by the country's doctors over a medical insurance dispute.

West Germany procures the release of 2,600 political prisoners from East Germany.

USSR Soviet writers Yuli Daniel and Andrei Sinyavsky are sentenced to five and seven years respectively, for 'anti-Soviet' writings.

Syria A group of army officers stages a successful, intra-party coup; President Hafiz is imprisoned, the cabinet is dissolved, the provisional constitution is abrogated and a regionalist, civilian Ba'ath government is introduced. The coup leaders described it as a 'rectification' of Ba'ath Party principles.

Uganda Milton Obote suspends the constitution and declares himself president, deposing King Mutesa II of Buganda.

Ghana A military coup overthrows President Kwame Nkrumah while he is abroad; sacked general, Joseph Ankrah comes to power.

Japan An All-Nippon Airways flight crashes into Tokyo Bay, killing 133.

Indonesia A curfew is imposed.

Australia The Australian dollar is introduced; initially there are two dollars to a pound.

••

Science & Technology: The Russian spacecraft, *Luna 9,* is the first craft to make a soft landing on the Moon.

Born: Cindy Crawford, US model and actress. Billy Zane, US actor.

Died: Buster Keaton, US actor and director, 70. Chester W. Nimitz, US World War II admiral, 80.

••

March

United Kingdom The Labour Party, led by incumbent prime minister Harold Wilson, wins the general election with an increased majority. The first official meeting for 400 years takes place between the Catholic and the Anglican churches.

Ireland An IRA bomb destroys Nelson's Column in Dublin.

France President de Gaulle announces that French troops will be withdrawn from NATO and that all French NATO bases and HQs must be closed within a year.

Spain The lost US hydrogen bomb is found in the Mediterranean sea off Palomares.

Belgium Paul Vanden Boeynants, leader of the PSC-CVP, is elected prime minister, replacing Pierre Harmel.

Netherlands Crown Princess Beatrix of the Netherlands marries Claus von Amsberg; there are demonstrations at the wedding because the groom is German.

USSR Leonid Brezhnev becomes first secretary of the Russian Communist Party; he denounces American policy in Vietnam, describing it as a policy of aggression.

USA Three men are convicted of the murder of Malcolm X.

11 March 1966
USA LSD advocate Timothy Leary is sentenced to 30 years in jail for trying to cross into Mexico while in possession of a small amount of marijuana. Sandoz, the pharmaceutical company that invented LSD stops supplying it to LSD researchers after the drug is heavily criticized in the media.

Guatemala 32 people are arrested on suspicion of helping Marxist guerrillas; they are never seen again.

Ecuador General Telmo Vargas overthrows the military junta of Ramón Castro Jijón; Clemente Yerovi is appointed interim president.

Uruguay Alberto Héber Usher becomes president.

China An earthquake in the area of the Chinese city of Xingtai kills around 8,000.

South Vietnam There are 215,000 US troops in Vietnam; B-52s begin bombing North Vietnam. 20,000 Buddhists march in protest at the policies of the government. Anti-Vietnam War protests take place in the United States, Europe and Australia.

Australia announces it will substantially increase its troops in Vietnam.

•••

Entertainment: The rock group, Buffalo Springfield is formed, with Neil Young and Steven Stills as members. John Lennon comments in an interview in the London *Evening Standard* that the Beatles are more popular than Jesus.

Science & Technology: Russia crashes *Venera 3*, on Venus; it is the first man-made object on the planet's surface. The Russian space probe *Luna 10* is the first spacecraft to go into orbit around the Moon.

20 March 1966
Sport: The World Cup trophy, the Jules Rimet trophy, is stolen from a rare-stamp exhibition in Westminster Hall in London, four months before the start of the tournament in England. The trophy is found by a dog named Pickles seven days later under a garden hedge in South London.

Died: Anna Akhmatova, Russian poet, 77. William Waldorf Astor, third Viscount Astor, British politician, 58. Maxfield Parrish, US artist, 95. Abe Saperstein, US founder of the Harlem Globetrotters, 63.

•••

April

United Kingdom The State Opening of Parliament is televised for the first time. A regular hovercraft service begins across the English Channel.

Rhodesia Prime minister, Ian Smith, severs diplomatic relations with Britain; the British government is given permission by the United

Nations to use force to stop oil tankers violating the embargo. Security forces kill seven members of the Zimbabwe African National Liberation Army (ZANLA) men in combat; 'Chimurenga' – the Zimbabwe African National Union (ZANU) rebellion – begins.

Iraq President Abdul Salam Arif dies in a helicopter crash; his brother, Abdul Rahman Arif becomes president.

El Salvador Military dictator, Maximiliano Hernandez Martinez, is assassinated; at 83, he is one of the oldest politicians to be assassinated.

Jamaica Ethiopian Emperor, Haile Selassie, who is worshipped by Rastafarians, is welcomed by huge crowds to the island.

Vietnam There are now 250,000 US troops in the country.

• •

Entertainment: The Grateful Dead move to San Francisco from Menlo County.

Science & Technology: The first Left Ventricular Assist Device (LVAD) is inserted in a patient in a cardiogenic shock postcardiotomy.

Born: John Daly, US golfer. Chris Evans, British broadcaster. Teddy Sheringham, British footballer. Phil Tuffnel, English cricketer and broadcaster.

Died: C. S. Forester, British author, 66. Flann O'Brien, Irish humorist, 54. Evelyn Waugh, British author, 63.

• •

May

United Kingdom A seamen's strike begins, aimed at securing higher wages and a reduction in the working week from 56 to 40 hours; the political importance of the strike is enormous: the disruption of trade has an adverse effect on the United Kingdom's precarious balance of payments, provoking a run on the pound and threatening to undermine the government's attempts to keep wage increases below 3.5 per cent; on 23 May, the government declares a state of emergency, although emergency powers are not used. The trial of the 'Moors Murderers' ends; Ian Brady is found guilty on all three counts of murder and sentenced to three concurrent terms of life imprisonment; Myra Hindley is convicted on two counts of murder and of being an accessory in the third murder; she receives two concurrent terms of life imprisonment and a seven-year fixed term for being an accessory.

Finland There are serious floods in the south of the country.

Nigeria The government forbids all political activity; the ban will last until 1969.

Rhodesia African members of the UN Security Council demand that the British army blockades Rhodesia.

USA Stokley Carmichael, credited with the coining of the term 'Black Power' is elected chairman of the Student Non-Violent Coordinating Committee (SNCC).

Cuba Fearing a US attack, Fidel Castro declares martial law.

Guyana declares independence from Britain.

Peru 248 football fans die in fights at a match between Peru and Argentina.

China Chairman Mao Zedong launches the Cultural Revolution, believing that liberal bourgeoisie elements are taking over the party and insisting that they need to be removed through post-revolutionary class struggle by mobilizing the thoughts and actions of China's youth, who formed Red Guards groups around the country; anarchy and terror ensues until 1976.

Vietnam Troops kill 80 protesting Buddhists. The South Vietnamese army besieges Da Nang.

Indonesia The Indonesian and Malayan governments declare the end of the Indonesian Confrontation.

Entertainment: The Beatles play their last British concert at the Empire Pool, Wembley. Bob Dylan releases his double album, *Blonde on Blonde*; while playing at Manchester Free Trade Hall, a member of the audience shouts 'Judas' in protest at Dylan's use of electric guitars and his abandoning of the folk idiom. The Beach Boys release their album *Pet Sounds*.

Born: Heston Blumenthal, British chef. Eric Cantona, French footballer and actor. Helena Bonham Carter, British actress. Jonathan Edwards, British athlete and broadcaster. Graham Hick, English cricketer. Janet Jackson, US singer.

Died: Jean Arp, German-French artist, 79. Tui Malila, a giant Galapagos land tortoise given by Captain James Cook to the Queen of Tonga in the 1770s, aged approximately 193.

June

The World This month, the period of relative peace following World War II will exceed that following World War I.

Ireland Eamon de Valera is re-elected as president.

France formally leaves NATO.

Vatican The *Index Librorum Prohibitorum* – Index of Banned Books – introduced in 1559 – is abolished.

Democratic Republic of the Congo Four former cabinet ministers are executed for allegedly plotting to kill President Mobutu.

USA Stokley Carmichael launches the Black Power movement.

Argentina General Julio Alsogaray, with the support of the army, the US government, the media and politicians such as former president ,Arturo Frondizi, stages a military coup, ousting President Illia; General Juan Carlos Ongania replaces him as president and rules as an authoritarian dictator.

China Mayor of Beijing, Peng Zhen, is hounded from office by Red Guards after being accused of turning the city into a personal empire. University entrance exams are postponed for six months in order to re-model the education system; schools and universities are closed throughout the country as students devote themselves to Red Guard activities.

North Vietnam US planes begin bombing Hanoi and Haiphong.

Australia Opposition leader Arthur Calwell is shot and wounded after attending a political meeting in Sydney.

Entertainment: The film *A Man for All Seasons* starring Paul Scofield wins six Academy Awards.

Science & Technology: US space probe, *Surveyor 1*, transmits detailed photographs from the lunar surface.

Born: John Cusack, US actor. Mike Tyson, US boxer.

July

United Kingdom The seamen's strike finally comes to an end. The first Plaid Cymru – Welsh nationalist – MP is elected to Parliament. England win the FIFA World Cup.

Syria Syrian Air Force jet fighters clash with Israeli fighters over the Jordan River.

Democratic Republic of the Congo Katangese troops revolt for several weeks in Stanleyville in support of exiled prime minister, Moise Tshombe.

The eighth staging of the FIFA World Cup was held in England from 11 to 30 July 1966. England were chosen as the hosts to celebrate the centenary of the codification of football in England. England beat West Germay 4-2 in the final, giving them their first (and only to this date) World Cup win, becoming the first host nation to win the tournament since Italy in 1934. The victorious British team were Bobby Moore (captain), George Cohen, Alan Ball, Roger Hunt, Ray Wilson, Nobby Stiles, Gordon Banks, Geoff Hurst, Bobby Charlton, Martin Peters and Jack Charlton. The venue for the final was London's Wembley Stadium, and 98,000 people crammed inside to watch the epic match. BBC commentator, Kenneth Wolstenholme's description of the match's closing moments has gone down in history – 'Some people are on the pitch. They think it's all over . . . [Hurst scores] . . . It is now!'

Malawi becomes a republic; Hastings Kamuzu Banda becomes president; he eventually declares a one-party state with himself as president for life.

Burundi King Mwambutsa IV Bangiriceng of Burundi is deposed by his son Ntare V, who is in turn deposed by Prime Minister Michel Micombero who declares a republic, naming himself president.

Zambia threatens to leave the Commonwealth following British peace moves towards Rhodesia.

USA The Supreme Court issues its decision that criminal suspects must be informed of their constitutional rights before being questioned. Race riots break out in Chicago. A state of emergency is declared in Cleveland following race riots. Richard Speck murders 8 student nurses in a Chicago dormitory.

Dominican Republic Joaquín Balaguer becomes president for the second of three times; he rules for 12 years during which schools, hospitals, dams, roads and public buildings are constructed and there is steady economic growth; his government is autocratic, however.

Bolivia Anti-communist, pro-free market politician Rene Barrientos is elected president.

Guatemala Julio César Méndez Montenegro of the Revolutionary Party becomes president.

Vietnam US B-52s bomb the demilitarized zone between North and South Vietnam for the first time.

North Vietnam declares a general mobilization. A Warsaw Pact meeting ends with a promise of support for North Vietnam.

Entertainment: The Beatles are attacked in the Philippines after insulting the president's wife, Imelda Marcos. Bob Dylan is injured in a motorcycle crash; he withdraws from performing and recording for a time to recover.

Sport: England wins the 1966 World Cup, beating Germany 4-2 in the final after extra time.

Born: Gianfranco Zola, Italian footballer and manager.

Died: Montgomery Clift, US actor, 45. Tony Lema, US golfer, 32. D. T. Suzuki, Japanese Zen Buddhism scholar, 96.

August

Turkey 2,400 die in an earthquake at Varko.

Nigeria General Yakubu Gowon has President Aguiyi-Ironsi machine-gunned to death by his troops, seizes power and becomes president.

Egypt Seven men are sentenced to death for anti-Nasser activities. Syria clashes with Israel for three hours on their common border at the Sea of Galilee.

French Somaliland Following riots, France promises independence; it becomes the French Territory of the Afars and the Issas and in 1977 will gain full independence as Djibouti.

Yemen Saudi Arabia and the United Arab Republic begin negotiations in Kuwait to end the war in Yemen.

USA There are widespread anti-war demonstrations across the country. Charles Whitman, an architecture and engineering student, shoots and kills 14 people from a tower at the University of Texas.

Nicaragua On the death of President René Schick Gutierrez, his relative, Lorenzo Guerrero Gutierrez, takes office.

Colombia Liberal Party leader Carlos Lleras Restrepo is elected president.

China The Cultural Revolution continues; 2,000 Beijing residents are estimated to have died in a two-week period.

Entertainment: There is outrage when John Lennon's comment that the Beatles are 'more popular than Jesus' is reprinted in the United States five months after he said it; South African Broadcasting bans Beatles records; the group is pelted with rotten fruit at a concert in Memphis; their records are burned in America's south; they play their last live concert at Candlestick Park, San Francisco.

> **❝ *Christianity will go. It will vanish and shrink. I needn't argue with that; I'm right and I will be proved right. We're more popular than Jesus now; I don't know which will go first – rock 'n' roll or Christianity.* ❞**

John Lennon

Science & Technology: The United States launches *Pioneer 7* into orbit.

Sport: Sir Francis Chichester sets out on his solo voyage around the world.

Born: Halle Berry, US actress. Les Ferdinand, English footballer.

Died: Lenny Bruce, US comedian, 41.

....

September

United Nations Secretary General U Thant says he will not seek re-election following his failure to secure peace in Vietnam.

United Kingdom 98 British tourists die in an air crash at Ljubljana, Yugoslavia. After three years on the run, Ronald 'Buster' Edwards, one of the participants in the 1963 Great Train Robbery, is arrested and sentenced to 15 years in prison.

West Germany Nazi war criminals, Baldur von Schirach – head of the Hitler Youth – and Albert Speer, minister of armaments and war, are released from Spandau Prison.

Botswana gains independence from Britain; Seretse Khama, independence movement leader is elected president; he will be re-elected twice, dying in office in 1980.

South Africa The architect of apartheid, Hendrik Verwoerd, is stabbed to death by Dimitri Tsafendas during a parliamentary meeting; Tsafendas is later diagnosed as insane; John Vorster becomes the new South African prime minister.

USA Timothy Leary stages a press conference where he announces the launch of a new psychedelic religion, the League for Spiritual Discovery; in his speech, he uses the phrase 'Turn on, tune in, drop out'.

....

Entertainment: *Star Trek, The Monkees* and *Mission Impossible* are seen for the first time on US television. The Metropolitan Opera House opens at the Lincoln Center in New York City. The British supergroup, Cream, is formed consisting of guitarist Eric Clapton, drummer Ginger Baker and bass player Jack Bruce; they release the first of four studio albums, *Fresh Cream*.

September 1966
Entertainment: Musician, Jimmy Hendrix, changes the spelling of his Christian name to Jimi.

Born: Akishino, Princess of Japan. Adam Sandler, US actor.
Died: André Breton, French writer and founder of Surrealism, 70. Margaret Sanger, US birth control advocate, 83.

●●

October

United Kingdom 140 people, mostly schoolchildren, die when a coal waste landslide engulfs their school in Aberfan, south Wales.

November 1966
Entertainment:
Russian spy, George Blake, escapes from Wormwood Scrubs prison and is next seen in Moscow.

Spain demands that Britain stops military flights to Gibraltar; Britain refuses; Spain closes its border with Gibraltar to non-pedestrian traffic.

USSR throws out all Chinese students.

Basutoland An enclave, entirely surrounded by South Africa, gains independence from Britain as the Kingdom of Lesotho; Moshoeshoe II reigns but Joseph Leabua Jonathan wields the real power as prime minister.

Namibia The United Nations revokes South Africa's mandate; the South-West Africa People's Organization's (SWAPO) military wing, the People's Liberation Army of Namibia begins a guerrilla campaign against South Africa, infiltrating the territory from bases in Zambia.

USA Huey Newton and Bobby Seale found the Black Panther Party, in support of Black Power.

Vietnam Hanoi insists on the ending of US bombing before it will enter into peace talks; US bombers continue to bomb North Vietnamese targets.

Indonesia Following the failed 1965 coup, a military court in Jakarta sentences ex-foreign minister Subandrio to death; the sentence is commuted to life and he will eventually be released in 1995.

●●

Entertainment: Grace Slick performs with the Jefferson Airplane for the first time.

Medicine & Health: LSD is made illegal in the United States.

Science & Technology: Russia puts *Luna 12* into orbit around the Moon.

Born: Roman Abramovich, Russian oil billionaire and football club owner. Tony Adams, British footballer. David Cameron, British politician. George Weah, Liberian footballer and politician.

Died: Elizabeth Arden, Canadian-born beautician and cosmetics entrepreneur, 87. Alma Cogan, British singer, 34.

November

Ireland Sean Lemass retires after seven years as taoiseach; fellow Fianna Fáil minister, Jack Lynch, succeeds him.

Spain declares an amnesty for crimes committed during the Spanish Civil War, although in reality it only applies to those on the Fascist side.

Netherlands Anti-Revolutionary Party (ARP) leader, Jelle Zijlstra, replaces Jo Cals as prime minister.

Italy 113 die when the River Arno, in Florence, overflows; the flood causes widespread damage to the collection in the Uffizi Gallery; in Venice, flooding makes 5,000 homeless.

Togo The army crushes an attempted coup.

Rhodesia 38 African states demand that the United Kingdom uses force against the Rhodesian government.

USA Former film star, Ronald Reagan, is elected governor of California.

> 66 *Politics is just like show business. You have a hell of an opening, coast for a while, and then have a hell of a close.* 99
>
> Ronald Reagan

Barbados gains independence from Britain; Democratic Labour Party leader Errol Barrow is its first prime minister.

Ecuador Otto Arosemena Gómez is elected president; to allay concerns about his being a dangerous leftist, Arosemena names a cabinet that includes Liberals and even Conservatives.

Entertainment: The Beatles begin the recording sessions for their album, *Sgt Pepper's Lonely Hearts Club Band*.

November 1966
Entertainment: John Lennon meets Japanese artist, Yoko Ono, at the Indica Gallery in Mayfair, London.

Born: Jeff Buckley, US singer. David Schwimmer, US actor.

December

United Nations U Thant agrees to serve a second term as secretary-general after all.

United Kingdom Thieves steal eight paintings worth millions of pounds from Dulwich Art Gallery in London; amongst them are three by Rembrandt and three by Rubens; they are recovered a few days later.

West Germany Heading a new CDU/CSU-SPD alliance, Conservative politician Kurt Georg Kiesinger is elected chancellor.

Greece After three prime ministers fail to form a government, Greek banker, Ioannis Paraskevopoulos, heads a caretaker government. 217 die when the ferry *Heraklion* sinks in the Aegean Sea near Crete.

Rhodesia British prime minister, Harold Wilson, and Rhodesian prime minister, Ian Smith, hold talks on HMS *Tiger* in the Mediterranean; Wilson withdraws all previous offers and announces that he will agree to independence only after the establishment of a black majority government; the United Nations Security Council approves an oil embargo; South Africa refuses to join the trade embargo.

Macau There are anti-Portuguese demonstrations; a curfew is imposed.

Vietnam US planes bomb Hanoi, capital of North Korea, for the first time. There are 385,000 US troops in Vietnam; more than 5,000 have died in action during the previous year.

••

Science & Technology: Russian spacecraft, *Luna 13*, soft lands on the Moon.

Born: Sinéad O'Connor, Irish singer. Alberto 'La Bomba' Tomba, Italian skier. Kiefer Sutherland, Canadian actor. Dennis Wise, British footballer.

Died: Walt Disney, US animated film producer, actor, director and entrepreneur, 65.

••

HIGHLIGHTS OF 1966

MAJOR FILMS

A Man for All Seasons
Alfie
Au Hasard, Balthazar
Blowup
Born Free
Funeral in Berlin

Georgy Girl
The Good, the Bad and the Ugly
Those Magnificent Men in their
    Flying Machines
Who's Afraid of Virginia Woolf?

Elizabeth Taylor (Martha) and Richard Burton (George) perform a little
musical number for their guest George Segal (Nick) in *Who's
Afraid of Virginia Woolf?*

HIT RECORDS

God Only Knows The Beach Boys
Good Vibrations The Beach Boys
Last Train To Clarksville The Monkees
Reach Out I'll Be There The Four Tops
Strangers In the Night Frank Sinatra
Sunny Afternoon The Kinks
The Sounds Of Silence Simon & Garfunkel
These Boots Are Made for Walkin' Nancy Sinatra
This Ole Heart Of Mine The Isley Brothers
Wild Thing The Troggs

BEST-SELLING BOOKS

Death of a Naturalist Seamus Heaney
Funeral in Berlin Len Deighton
In Cold Blood Truman Capote
Octopussy and the *Living Daylights* Ian Fleming
The Jewel in the Crown Paul Scott
The Adventurers Harold Robbins
A Thousand Days, Arthur Schlesinger Jr
Valley of the Dolls Jacqueline Susann

FLOWER POWER
TAKES ROOT

1967

January

The World More than 60 nations sign a treaty banning nuclear weapons from space.

United Kingdom opens negotiations in Rome for membership of the European Economic Community. Jeremy Thorpe becomes leader of the Liberal Party. The new town of Milton Keynes is founded. In total, 90 per cent of the British steel industry is nationalized.

West Germany establishes diplomatic relations with Romania.

Togo 29-year-old Lieutenant-Colonel Etienne Eyadéma ousts President Grunitzky in a bloodless military coup; Eyadéma rules until 2005 to become Africa's longest-reigning ruler; the personality cult created around him will include an entourage of 1,000 dancing women, portraits in every shop and a depiction of him as a superhero in a comic book.

Nigeria The military leaders and senior police officials of each region meet in Aburi, Ghana and agree on a loose confederation of regions.

January 1967
Canada The Expo '67 World Fair begins in Montreal, celebrating Canada's centenary. It is the most successful World Fair of the 20th century.

USA Jack Ruby, the killer of President Kennedy's assassin, Lee Harvey Oswald, dies of lung cancer in the same hospital in which Oswald died and in which President Kennedy was pronounced dead. Edward W. Brooke, the first black person elected to the US Senate by popular vote, takes his seat. Segregationist, Lestor Maddox is inaugurated as governor of Georgia. A draft board refuses a Vietnam exemption on religious grounds for boxer, Muhammad Ali. Albert DeSalvo, the 'Boston Strangler', is convicted of numerous murders and sentenced to life in prison.

Bahamas Sir Lynden Oscar Pindling becomes the first black prime minister of the Bahamas; he will become the longest-serving elected leader in the Western Hemisphere, ruling until 1992.

Bolivia Che Guevara begins organizing the National Liberation Army in Bolivia.

Vietnam 30,000 US and South Vietnamese troops launch a huge attack in the Mekong Delta.

Entertainment: To mark the de-legalizing of LSD, the first Human Be-In is held in San Francisco's Golden Gate Park, drawing national attention to

Haight-Ashbury and launching the 'Summer of Love'; Timothy Leary tells 20,000 people to 'Turn on, Tune in, Drop out. The poet Alan Ginsberg coins the term 'Flower Power'. The Doors release their eponymous first album. Charlie Chaplin's last film, *A Countess From Hong Kong*, opens in England.

FLOWER POWER

'Flower Power' was a slogan used by hippies during the late 1960s as a symbol of passive resistance and non-violence, and was rooted in opposition to the Vietnam War. The expression was coined by the American poet Allen Ginsberg to encourage war protestors to enact a non-violent revolution. Followers of 'Flower Power' dressed in clothing with embroidered flowers and vibrant colours, wore flower garlands in their hair and embraced the hippie culture.

Science & Technology: A launch pad fire at Cape Kennedy kills three astronauts – Gus Grissom, Edward White and Roger Chaffee – on board the US spacecraft, *Apollo 1*.

Sport: American Football's first Superbowl is won by Green Bay Packers. Donald Campbell is killed in a crash of his craft, *Bluebird*, while trying to break the world water-speed record on Coniston water in the Lake District, England.

Born: R. Kelly, US singer.

February

United Kingdom The extreme right party, the National Front, is founded; it opposes immigration and multiculturalism.

USSR announces that it has sent troops to the Chinese border. Soviet satellite states are banned from establishing diplomatic relations with West Germany.

Dominica gains independence from Britain.

Jamaica Prime Minister Alexander Bustamante is succeeded as premier by his deputy Donald Sangster.

Trinidad and Tobago become the first Commonwealth nation to join the Organization of American States.

Antigua and Barbuda Chief minister, Sir Vere Cornwall Bird Sr, becomes the first prime minister.

Tibet China sends three divisions of troops to Tibet.

China As tension mounts, the government announces it can no longer guarantee the safety of Soviet diplomats outside the Soviet Embassy.

Vietnam 13 US helicopters are shot down in one day. Near the Cambodian border, 25,000 American troops launch the biggest offensive of the war to date.

Australia Ronald Ryan is the last man to be hanged in Australia, for murdering a guard while escaping from prison in December 1965. 62 die in bushfires in Tasmania.

Entertainment: San Francisco band Jefferson Airplane release their seminal album, *Surrealistic Pillow*; it is one of the essential albums of the counter-culture hippie movement.

Sport: The American Basketball Association (ABA) is founded.

Born: Roberto Baggio, Italian footballer. Kurt Cobain, musician (Nirvana). Laura Dern, US actress. Benicio del Toro, Puerto Rican actor.

Died: Victor Gollancz, British publisher, 73. Henry Luce, US publisher and founder of *Time* magazine amongst others, 68. J. Robert Oppenheimer, US physicist and major figure in the development of the atomic bomb, 62.

March

United Kingdom The Queen Elizabeth Hall is opened in London. The first North Sea gas is pumped ashore at Easington, County Durham.

18 March 1967
United Kingdom The supertanker, *Torrey Canyon*, ran aground when it struck Pollard's Rock in the Seven Stones Reef between the Scilly Isles and Land's End. It was carrying a cargo of 120,000 tons of crude oil which spilled into the sea as the tanker began to break up. To try and avoid a major disaster, it was decided to bomb the tanker in an attempt to send it to the bottom of the sea and to burn off the oil which had already formed a slick 56 km (35 miles) long and up to 32 km (20 miles) wide. However, despite direct hits and a towering inferno of flames, the tanker refused to sink. The mission had to be called off when particularly high spring tides put out the flames. The *Torrey Canyon* was finally sunk the following day and the oil slick was dispersed by favourable weather, but not before 112 km (70 miles) of Cornish coastline were seriously contaminated and tens of thousands of seabirds killed.

Greece The Aspida Case – 15 army officers are sentenced to between two and 18 years in prison, for treason and plotting a coup.

USSR The daughter of Josef Stalin, Svetlana Alliluyeva, defects to the West in India, denouncing her father's regime.

Democratic Republic of the Congo Former prime minister, Moise Tshombe, is sentenced to death *in absentia*.

Sierra Leone Four days after its first parliamentary elections since independence, the head of the army, Brigadier-General David Lansana, seizes power from newly elected Prime Minister Siaka Stevens; two days later, senior military officers overthrow Lansana and create a National Reformation Council (NRC); the Anti-Corruption Revolutionary Movement imprisons senior NRC members, restores the constitution and reinstates Stevens as prime minister.

USA President Johnson announces his plan for a lottery for conscription into the army. Teamsters Union leader, Jimmy Hoffa, begins an eight-year prison sentence for attempting to bribe a jury. Scientists claim that LSD causes chromosome damage; the claim is never validated.

Grenada gains partial independence from Britain.

China The Red Guards return to school.

Uruguay Óscar Diego Gestido of the Colorado Party succeeds Alberto Heber of the National Party as president.

Brazil Artur da Costa e Silva becomes the second president following the military coup of 1964; his government marks the most oppressive stage of the military regime against communists.

Indonesia The State Assembly strips Sukarno of his presidential powers after 22 years and names Suharto as president; he will rule for 32 years.

∙∙∙

Entertainment: The album *The Velvet Underground and Nico* is released; it has been recorded during Andy Warhol's Exploding Plastic Inevitable multimedia event tour; largely ignored on its release, it will become recognized for its experimentalism and controversial subject matter.

Medicine & Health: Nine executives of the German pharmaceutical company Grunenthal are charged for breaking German drug laws with their drug thalidomide which was taken by pregnant mothers and caused birth defects in children.

Science and Technology: France launches its first nuclear submarine.

Died: Nelson Eddy, US baritone and actor, 65. Alice B. Toklas, US personality and life partner of writer Gertrude Stein, 89.

∙∙∙

April

France Georges Pompidou becomes prime minister for the fourth time.

Netherlands KVP leader Piet de Jong replaces Jelle Zijlstra as prime minister.

Hungary Jenö Fock replaces Gyula Kállai as prime minister; he retains the position until 1975.

Greece Panagiotis Kanellopoulos briefly heads a caretaker government, from 3 to 21 April; on 21 April, 'The Colonels', led by Colonel George Papadopoulos, seize power in a bloodless military coup; Konstantinos Kollias becomes prime minister.

Cyprus A Globe Air Bristol Britannia turboprop crashes at Nicosia, Cyprus, killing 126 people.

Israel and Syria Border fighting breaks out; Israeli fighters shoot down seven Syrian MiG-21 jet fighters.

Swaziland is granted internal self-government by Britain.

Aden A United Nations delegation accuses British authorities of a lack of cooperation; the British claim the delegation failed to contact them.

Canada Montreal's Expo 67 opens; 62 nations participate and 50 million visitors will pass through its gates before it closes in October.

USA There are large demonstrations against the Vietnam War in San Francisco and New York where 400,000 march from Central Park to the United Nations.

Jamaica Prime Minister Donald Sangster dies in office; Hugh Shearer becomes prime minister.

Cuba Fidel Castro declares that intellectual property belongs to everyone and that Cuba will translate and publish technical literature without paying compensation to its authors.

∙∙∙

Science & Technology: The first Boeing 737 makes its maiden flight. *Surveyor 3* lands on the Moon. Vladimir Komarov is the first Soviet cosmonaut to die, when the parachute of his space capsule, *Soyuz 1,* fails during re-entry.

Sport: Muhammad Ali refuses to be inducted into the US Army; he is stripped of his World Heavyweight title.

Born: Noel Gallagher, British musician (Oasis). Prince Willem-Alexander of the Netherlands, heir-apparent to the Dutch throne.

Died: Konrad Adenauer, former West German chancellor, 91.

∙∙∙

May

United Kingdom re-applies to join the European Community; General de Gaulle of France again vetoes entry.

Belgium 323 die in a fire at the *L'Innovation* department store in the centre of Brussels; many of the victims are women and children; the cause is unknown but there is suspicion that the fire has been started as a protest at the American goods sold in the store and against the Vietnam War.

Greece The Greek military government accuses imprisoned former prime minister Andreas Papandreou of treason.

USSR Yuri Andropov becomes head of the KGB.

Egypt President Nasser demands the withdrawal of the UN Emergency Peacekeeping Force from Sinai; U.N. Secretary-General U Thant complies; Nasser closes the Straits of Tiran to Israeli shipping, blockading the southern Israeli port of Eilat; he moves 9,000 men, 200 tanks and guns to positions at the edge of the Gaza Strip, near Rafah; he postpones his military attack due for the 28 May, fearing US intervention and unsure of Soviet support; he signs a pact with Jordan and Iraq allowing Jordanian forces to be put under Egyptian military command.

Syria mobilizes its forces against Israel.

Nigeria The military Governor of the Eastern Region of Nigeria, Chukwuemeka Odumegwu Ojukwu, announces that it is seceding from Nigeria and will henceforth be known as the Republic of Biafra; the area is responsible for the majority of Nigeria's oil exports; the ensuing war lasts two years, creates a humanitarian disaster and claims a million lives.

India Dr Zakir Hussain becomes the first Muslim President of India.

Nicaragua General Anastasio 'Tachito' Somoza Debayle becomes president; he rules until 1979 and is the last member of the Somoza family to be president; the family has been in power since 1936.

Hong Kong 51 striking workers die in riots.

Australia A referendum is passed with an overwhelming 90 per cent support removing from the Australian Constitution two discriminatory sentences referring to Indigenous Australians; it marks the beginning of Australia's recognition of rights for its indigenous people.

May 1967
Entertainment: Elvis Presley marries 21-year-old Priscilla Beaulieu in Las Vegas. The couple met in West Germany in 1959, where Presley was serving his time in the army. Their only daughter, Lisa Marie, was born in February 1968.

Entertainment: The Beatles release their album *Sgt Pepper's Lonely Hearts Club Band*; it remains at number one in Britain for 27 weeks and in America for 19; the BBC bans the song, *A Day in the Life* because of drug references; Paul McCartney announces that the Beatles have taken acid – LSD. The king of daredevils, motorcyclist, Evel Knievel jumps 16 cars on his motorbike at Ascot Speedway. This jump was the first of many to be covered by ABC's Wide World of Sports. *Mister Rogers' Neighborhood*, the longest-running children's series on US television, airs its first episode.

Sport: Celtic becomes the first British team to win the European Cup, beating Inter Milan 2–1 in the final. Francis Chichester arrives home from the first solo circumnavigation of the world on board *Gypsy Moth IV*; he is knighted. The International Olympic Committee bans a number of substances including narcotics, steroids and amphetamines; small-scale drug-testing will begin at the 1968 Olympics in Grenoble and Mexico City.

Science & Technology: Britain's first satellite *Ariel III* goes into orbit.

Born: Nicole Kidman, Australian actress.

Died: Edward Hopper, US painter, 85. J. Langston Hughes, US poet laureate and author, 65. John Masefield, British poet, 88.

June

United Kingdom A British Midland flight crashes in Hopes Carr, Stockport, killing all 72 passengers and crew. *On the Buses* star, Reg Varney, becomes the first person to use an Automatic Teller Machine (ATM or cashpoint) outside a branch of Barclays in Enfield, North London.

Denmark The heir to the Danish throne, Margrethe, marries French count Henri de Laborde de Monpezat.

Vatican The Pope ordains Karol Wojtyla, the future Pope John Paul II, as a cardinal.

USSR severs diplomatic relations with Israel.

The Middle East The Six Day War breaks out; Israel, convinced that an Arab attack is imminent, raids Egyptian military targets; Syria, Jordan and Iraq also enter the conflict; Jordan loses the 5,879 sq km (2,270 sq miles) of the West Bank; Israel also captures the Golan Heights, the Gaza Strip and east Jerusalem, including the Wailing Wall; a United Nations-mediated cease-fire is accepted by Israel and Egypt on 10 June. Israel annexes east Jerusalem and declares the city reunified in retaliation for Jordan's participation in the war.

Democratic Republic of the Congo President Mobutu centralizes all power in his office, effectively becoming dictator. Former prime minister, Moise Tshombe, is kidnapped while in exile in Algeria.

USA 14 people are shot during a race riot in Buffalo. The Summer of Love begins in San Francisco.

Vietnam There are now 448,400 US troops in Vietnam.

∙∙

Entertainment: The Beatles perform the song *All You Need is Love* to a global audience during One World, the first live, international satellite television broadcast. The three-day Monterey Pop Festival features the first US performances by The Who and Jimi Hendrix and the first major appearances by Janis Joplin and Otis Redding.

Science & Technology: The USA launches the space probe *Venera 4* which will be the first craft to enter another planet's atmosphere and return data. China tests its first hydrogen bomb.

Sport: Muhammad Ali is sentenced to five years imprisonment for draft evasion.

Born: Pamela Anderson, Canadian actress.

Died: Jayne Mansfield, US actor, 34. Dorothy Parker, US author, 73. Spencer Tracy, US actor, 67.

∙∙

July

United Kingdom The Sexual Offences Act is passed; homosexuality is decriminalized between consenting adults aged 21 or over. The British steel industry is nationalized. BBC2 makes the first UK colour television broadcast – a tennis match from Wimbledon. To the disapproval of the United States and Australia, Britain announces the closure of its bases in Malaysia and Singapore.

East Germany 94 die, mostly children, when a train collides with a truck near Magdeburg.

Greece The Greek military government strips almost 500 people of their citizenship.

Morocco Mohamed Benhima becomes prime minister.

Democratic Republic of the Congo Belgian colonial and farmer, Jean Schramme, leads a rebellion in the province of Katanga; he will finally be defeated at the end of October.

Canada celebrates its centenary. General de Gaulle causes controversy when he declares during a visit to Montreal, 'Vive le Quebec libre!' (Long live free Quebec!).

> ## 66 *A true leader always keeps an element of surprise up his sleeve, which others cannot grasp but which keeps his public excited and breathless.* 99
>
> Charles de Gaulle

USA The Freedom of Information Act becomes law, making government information available to the public. A long hot summer of race riots begins; 27 die in Newark, 40 in Detroit where 5,000 are left homeless. 37 die in a prison riot in Florida. 134 sailors die in an explosion and fire on USS *Forrestal* in the Gulf of Tonkin off Vietnam; it occurs when a rocket on a fighter plane misfires, hitting the external tank of another aircraft; 161 are injured, 21 aircraft are destroyed and the total cost is estimated at $72 million. Black Panther H. Rap Brown is arrested in Maryland for inciting a riot.

El Salvador Fidel Sánchez Hernández becomes president, continuing his predecessor's progressive reform but ruling during a time of war and economic turmoil.

Venezuela 240 die in an earthquake at Caracas.

Japan Following heavy rain, 371 people die in a landslide at the cities of Kobe and Kure.

Vietnam General William Westmoreland claims that America is winning the war, but says that he needs more men.

July 1967
Entertainment: The British pop group, Pink Floyd's, debut album *The Piper at the Gates of Dawn* is released, reaching number six in the UK album charts. (l to r) Roger Waters, Nick Mason, Syd Barrett and Richard Wright.

> **❝** *When the power of love overcomes the love of power the world will know peace... When things get too heavy, just call me helium, the lightest known gas to man ... Imagination is the key to my lyrics. The rest is painted with a little science fiction.* **❞**
>
> Jimi Hendrix

Born: Will Ferrell, US actor.

Died: John Coltrane, US jazz composer and musician, 41. Alfred Kruup, German industrialist, 59. Vivien Leigh, British actor, 53. Albert Luthuli, South African Nobel Prize-winning President of the ANC, 69. Basil Rathbone, British actor, 75. Carl Sandburg, US poet, 89. Tommy Simpson, British cyclist, 29.

August

United Kingdom Pirate radio stations are made illegal in the Marine Broadcasting Offences Act.

India Madras State is re-named Tamil Nadu.

USA Race riots spread to Washington DC. The leader of the American Nazi Party, George Lincoln Rockwell, is assassinated in Arlington, Virginia; a member of his organization, the National Socialist White People's Party, John Patler, is found guilty of his murder. Thurgood Marshall becomes the first African American justice of the United States Supreme Court. Abbie Hoffman and the Yippies throw hundreds of dollar bills onto the floor of the New York Stock Exchange, causing chaos.

Grenada Labour politician, Eric Matthew Gairy, becomes the country's first prime minister; he will lead the country until 1979.

Southeast Asia The Association of Southeast Asian Nations (ASEAN) is formed by Indonesia, Malaysia, the Philippines, Singapore and Thailand.

Vietnam President Johnson announces that he is sending 45,000 more troops to Vietnam.

Science & Technology: British scientists Jocelyn Bell and Antony Hewish record the discovery of the pulsar. 'An entirely novel kind of star came to light on August 6...' Hewish will receive a Nobel Prize for it.

Born: Ulrika Jonsson, Swedish television presenter.

Died: Stanley Bruce, former prime minister of Australia, 84. Charles Darrow, US inventor of Monopoly, 78. Brian Epstein, British manager of the Beatles, 32. René Magritte, Belgian painter, 68. Joe Orton, British actor and playwright, 34.

....

September

United Kingdom The BBC launches Radio One, Two, Three and Four. The passenger ship, *Queen Elizabeth II* (QE2) is launched by the Queen; she uses the same pair of gold scissors used by her mother and grandmother to launch the *Queen Elizabeth* and *Queen Mary*, respectively.

Gibraltar In a referendum, only 44 out of 12,182 voters support a union with Spain.

West Germany Imprisoned Nazi war criminal, Ilse Koch, known as the 'Witch of Buchenwald', commits suicide in a Bavarian prison.

Sweden Motorists begin driving on the right, instead of the left.

Greece The Greek Colonels release former prime minister, Georgios Papandreou, from prison following pressure from the United States.

Turkey 44 die in a riot at a football match in Kayseri.

USSR signs an agreement to send more aid to North Vietnam.

Nigeria Fighting continues against Biafra.

South Vietnam Lieutenant General Nguyen Van Thieu is elected president; he gains a reputation for corruption.

North Vietnam rejects a US peace proposal. Operation Swift begins. U.S. Marines launch a search-and-destroy mission in Quang Nam and Quang Tin Provinces. The ensuing four-day battle in Que Son Valley kills 114 Americans and 376 North Vietnamese.

....

Born: Harry Connick Jr, US singer and actor. Macy Gray, US singer. Michael Johnson, US athlete. Mira Sorvino, US actress. Moon Unit Zappa, US singer and daughter of Frank Zappa.

Died: Siegfried Sassoon, British poet, 81. Prince Felix Yusupov, Russian assassin of Rasputin, 80.

....

October

United Kingdom French president, de Gaulle, again vetoes Britain's entry into the EEC. The breathalyzer is introduced. Parliament passes an abortion bill clarifying the law on abortion; a woman is legally allowed to have an abortion on a number of grounds. The Kray twins murder London criminal Jack 'the Hat' McVitie; it will lead to their eventual imprisonment.

Egypt An Egyptian missile sinks the Israeli destroyer *Eilat*, 47 sailors die; Israel retaliates by shelling Egyptian refineries along the Suez Canal.

Iran The Shah crowns himself and his queen in an extravagant ceremony; he has been on the Peacock Throne for 26 years.

India A powerful cyclone wipes out all life in the rural state of Orissa; the number of casualties is huge but unknown.

Brunei Sultan Omar Ali Saifuddin III abdicates; the 29th sultan, Haji Hassanal Bolkiah Mu'Izzaddin Waddaulah, takes the throne.

USA 50,000 anti-war protestors march in Washington; poet Allen Ginsberg symbolically attempts to levitate the Pentagon by chanting. Future senator and presidential candidate John McCain is shot down over North Vietnam; he will be a prisoner for five years.

Bolivia Che Guevara is captured and executed by US-trained Bolivian troops near Vado del Yeso.

Hong Kong British and Chinese troops clash along the Hong Kong-Chinese border.

Entertainment: The musical, *Hair*, opens off-Broadway. Walt Disney's *The Jungle Book* is released; it becomes a huge success.

HAIR – THE MUSICAL

Hair told the story of a group of long-haired 'Hippies of the Age of Aquarius' who were fighting against conscription to the Vietnam War, and living the bohemian lifestyle together in New York City. When the musical opened in 1967, it got off to a very shaky start and its first two runs were cut short. Producer Michael Butler and director Tom O'Horgan were brought in to rescue the show, and it took three months to revamp the musical. When it finally appeared at the Biltmore on Broadway it had 19 songs in the first act, compared with just nine in the original production.

Hair opened at the Shafesbury Theatre in London the following year, on the 27 September 1968, just one day after the abolition of theatre censorship. Some scenes in the musical, written by actors Gerome Ragni and James Rado, would have previously been considered too outrageous to be shown on a stage in Britain. Many people were angered by scenes containing nudity and drug-taking, as well as the strong anti-war message at the height of the Vietnam conflict. The original London cast included Sonja Kristina, Paul Nicholas, Richard O'Brien, Melba Moore, Elaine Paige, Paul Korda, Marsha Hunt, Floella Benjamin, Alex Harvey, Oliver Tobias and Tim Curry. *Hair's* London production surpassed the Broadway show, running for 1,997 performances until its closure was forced by the roof collapsing in July 1973.

Science & Technology: A Russian unmanned spacecraft makes the first landing on Venus. US probe *Mariner 5* flies by Venus.

Born: Julia Roberts, US actress.

Died: Clement Atlee, former British prime minister, 84. Che Guevara, Argentinean revolutionary, 39. Woody Guthrie, US folksinger and composer, 55. Aisin-Gioro Henry Puyi, last emperor of China, 61. Sir Malcolm Sargent, British conductor, 72.

November

United Nations The Security Council approves Resolution 242 calling on Israel to withdraw from the territories it captured during 1967's Six Day War; it also implicitly calls on Israel's enemies to recognize its existence.

United Kingdom Chancellor James Callaghan devalues the pound by 14 per cent. Another application for entry to the Common Market is vetoed by France's president de Gaulle. A train derails at Hither Green, killing 49. The BBC launches its first local radio station, Radio Leicester.

Portugal Floods following a cloudburst over Lisbon kill 450 people.

Cyprus General Grivas and his 10,000 Greek troops are forced to leave Cyprus after 24 Turkish Cypriots are killed in the villages of Kophinou and Ayios Theodhoros; relations between Greece and Turkey become even more strained.

Pakistan Zulfiqar Ali Bhutto founds the Pakistan People's Party and becomes its first chairman; it will become one of the country's main political parties.

South Yemen gains independence from Britain; Qahtan ash-Sha'abi is the first president.

Rhodesia passes pro-Apartheid laws.

USA Carl Stokes is elected mayor of Cleveland; he is the first black mayor of a major American city. Secretary of Defence, Robert McNamara, resigns to become president of the World Bank.

Bolivia French author, Regis Debray is sentenced to 30 years in prison for being part of Che Guevara's guerrilla group; he will be freed in 1970 after an international campaign for his release.

Vietnam 365 Viet Cong die in a huge battle in the Mekong Delta.

Entertainment: The BBC bans *I Am the Walrus* by the Beatles. The Los Angeles band Love release their classic album *Forever Changes*. The Moody Blues album *Days of Future Passed* is released. The first issue of *Rolling Stone* magazine is published.

Science & Technology: The US craft, *Surveyor 6,* makes the first lift-off from the surface of the Moon.

Born: Judd Apatow, US screenwriter and director. Boris Becker, West German tennis player. Jamie Foxx, US actor.

December

United Kingdom The BBC begins a full colour television service. The cruise liner *Queen Mary* is retired from service.

Romania Nicolae Ceausescu becomes president, as well as leader of the Communist Party.

Greece The military junta crushes an attempted counter rebellion led by King Constantine II; the royal family flees the country and the monarchy will be abolished in 1973; Georgios Papadopoulos, leader of the April coup replaces Konstantinos Kollias as prime minister.

Cyprus A Turkish-Cypriot government is formed.

Israel submits a five-year plan to solve the Arab refugee problem, conditional on a peace agreement with the Arab states.

Gabon President Leon M'Ba dies; Omar Bongo succeeds as president; as of May 2009 he is still in power as the world's longest-serving ruler, outside monarchies.

Uruguay President Óscar Gestido is the third Uruguayan president to die in office in 20 years; Jorge Pacheco Areco becomes president.

Vietnam There are 474,300 US troops in Vietnam. 60 per cent of the 15,000 US troops killed in the war so far have died in 1967.

Australia Prime Minister Harold Holt disappears while swimming at a beach near Melbourne; John 'Black Jack' McEwen becomes prime minister.

Entertainment: As the music world goes psychedelic, Bob Dylan releases his country album *John Wesley Harding*.

Medicine & Health: In South Africa, surgeons, led by Dr Christiaan Barnard, perform the first human heart transplant; the patient Louis Washkansky lives for 18 days. DNA is created in a test tube for the first time.

Science & Technology: Professor John Archibald Wheeler, one of Albert Einstein's later collaborators, uses the term Black Hole for the first time while delivering a talk at the NASA Goddard Institute of Space Studies.

December 1967
Science & Technology: The world's first supersonic airliner, the British–French Concorde, is unveiled in Toulouse.

Died: Bert Lahr, US actor, 72. Otis Redding US singer, 26. Paul Whiteman, US band leader, 77.

HIGHLIGHTS OF 1967

MAJOR FILMS

Bonnie and Clyde
Camelot
Cool Hand Luke
Doctor Dolittle
*Guess Who's
    Coming to Dinner*
*In the Heat of the
    Night*
The Dirty Dozen
The Graduate
The Jungle Book
To Sir, With Love

Dustin Hoffman
(Benjamin Braddock)
and Anne Bancroft
(Mrs Robinson) in *The
Graduate*, directed by
Mike Nichols

HIT RECORDS

A Whiter Shade Of Pale Procol Harum
All You Need Is Love The Beatles
Happy Together The Turtles
I Heard It Through The Grapevine Gladys Knight and the Pips
I Was Made To Love Her Stevie Wonder
I'm a Believer The Monkees
Light My Fire The Doors
Puppet On a String Sandie Shaw
Respect Aretha Franklin
San Francisco (Be Sure to Wear Flowers In Your Hair) Scott
    McKenzie

BEST-SELLING BOOKS

I'm OK, You're OK Thomas A. Harris MD
The Death of a President William Manchester
The Fixer Bernard Malamud
The Ghost in the Machine Arthur Koestler
The Mersey Sound Adrian Henri, Roger McGough and
    Brian Patten
The Owl Service Alan Garner
The Games People Play Eric Berne

ASSASSINATION
AND CIVIL UNREST

1968

January

United Kingdom Five typists set up the patriotic 'I'm Backing Britain' campaign aimed at giving a boost to the British economy; people are asked to work an extra half day a week without pay; after several months it fizzles out without making any appreciable difference. Twenty people die in a hurricane that rampages across central Scotland.

Italy An earthquake in Sicily kills 231 people.

Czechoslovakia Alexander Dubček replaces Antonín Novotný as first secretary of the Czech Communist party, the first step towards what will become known as the Prague Spring.

Panama Dr Arnulfo Arias Madrid becomes president for the third time but after 11 days he is ousted by a military coup; each of his three presidencies has ended in the same manner; José María Pinilla Fábrega assumes chairmanship of the provisional ruling junta.

North Korea seizes technical research ship, the USS *Pueblo*, claiming the ship has violated its territorial waters while spying; the United States later claims that it has been captured by order of the Soviet Union which wants to get its hands on a cryptographic machine that is onboard so they can match it with a key provided to them by the spy John Walker; the crew is released, but the ship remains in North Korea to this day.

January 1968
Vietnam US bombing targets shift from North Vietnam to Laos. The Battle of Khe Sanh begins, lasting two and a half months. It is the longest and bloodiest battle of the war. The North Vietnamese launch the Tet Offensive, attacking more than 100 towns and cities in South Vietnam, including the US Embassy in Saigon, which was a major setback for US forces. The controversy surrounding this battle has continued long after the last gun was fired. Both sides claimed victory at Khe Sanh which many believe was just a diversionary tactic, fuelling a debate which continues today.

Nauru at 20.9 sq km (8.1 sq miles) in size, becomes the world's smallest nation when it declares independence from Australia; the South Pacific island, rich in phosphate, is led by Hammer DeRoburt as first president.

Australia The Liberals elect a new leader; John McEwan is replaced as prime minister by John Gorton.

• •

Entertainment: The television comedy show, *Rowan & Martin's Laugh-In* is shown for the first time. Johnny Cash records *Live at Folsom Prison*.

Sport: The Green Bay Packers win their third successive Superbowl, under coach Vince Lombardi in his last game in charge; the Superbowl trophy is re-named the Vince Lombardi Trophy.

Born: Cuba Gooding Jr, US actor. LL Cool J, US rapper and actor.

• •

February

United Kingdom adopts year-round daylight-saving time.

Denmark Hilmar Baunsgaard of the Social Liberal Party is elected prime minister, ending 15 years of government by the Social Democrats; he governs via a coalition with the Conservative Party and the Liberal Venstre Party.

Israel and Jordan border clashes break out.

USA Three students are killed by police at a civil rights protest at a whites-only bowling alley in Orangeburg, South Carolina. Segregationist Alabama governor, George Wallace, announces his candidacy for the presidency. Timothy Leary closes down the LSD research centre at Millbrook after countless FBI raids on the premises.

South Vietnam Martial law is declared after North Vietnamese troops occupy Tan Son Nhut airport in Saigon; Eddie Adams famously photographs Saigon's police chief, Nguyen Ngoc Loan executing a Viet Cong officer with a shot to the head. The Tet Offensive ends with the crushing of Viet Cong resistance in Hué; 142 marines die and 857 are wounded; Viet Cong losses are estimated at more than 5,000.

• •

Entertainment: The Beatles travel to India to study transcendental meditation with the Maharishi at Rishikesh on the Ganges. US singer Frankie Lymon, formerly lead singer in vocal group Frankie and the Teenagers is found dead in Harlem from a heroin overdose, aged 25.

• •

❝ *When a man has risen to cosmic consciousness, then his state is like that of an ever-full and steady ocean. This state of absolute bliss is the goal of all desires in life.* **❞**

Maharishi Mahesh Yogi from *Thirty Years Around the World*

• •

Science & Technology: The discovery of the first pulsar, a star that emits regular radio waves, is announced by Dr Jocelyn Bell Burnell at Cambridge University, England.

Sport: The 10th Winter Olympics are opened by President Charles de Gaulle in Grenoble, France.

Born: Lisa Marie Presley, US daughter of Elvis Presley and future wife of Michael Jackson.

Died: Neal Cassady, US beat writer and driver, 41.

March

United Kingdom Foreign Secretary George Brown resigns. 91 people are injured in a mass protest against the Vietnam War at the US Embassy in Grosvenor Square, London.

France Daniel Cohn-Bendit, known as 'Danny the Red' and seven other students occupy offices at the University of Nanterre, setting in motion the events that almost lead to revolution in May.

DANNY THE RED

Pictured here are French student leaders Jacques Sauvageot and Daniel Cohn-Bendit, better known as Danny the Red. Daniel was born in Montauban France on 4 April 1945 and was given the nickname Dany la Rouge or Danny the Red during his student years because of his politics and the colour of his hair. He moved to Germany in 1958 and at the age of 14 chose to take up German citizenship in order to avoid conscription. Daniel returned to France in 1966 to study sociology at the University of Nanterre where he quickly became known as the 'voice of the students'. He attracted a lot of supporters, later to be called the '22 March Movement', a group characterized by a mixture of Marxist, sexual and anarchist semantics. Because of his outspokenness, Daniel was almost expelled from the university, but rumours of a students' strike, meant that his expulsion was cancelled. On 22 March 1968, students occupied the administrative offices which forced the closing of the university, and the protestors moved to downtown Paris. From 3 May onwards, massive student riots eruped in Paris against Charles de Gaulle's government. Although Daniel played a relatively small part during the riots, he had become a legend, which was an advantage to him in his future career in politics.

Netherlands The green, left-wing Political Party Radikalen (PPR) is founded. The embassies of Greece, Spain and Portugal in The Hague are bombed.

Poland Major student and intellectual protests break out against the communist government, repression by the security services and the Soviet Union's anti-Zionist policy.

Czechoslovakia General Ludvik Svoboda is elected president of Czechoslovakia. The officials censoring printed materials seek permission to end their censorship.

Jordan Israeli forces attack a PLO base in response to attacks on northern Israel.

USA President Johnson announces he will not seek re-election. Senator Robert Kennedy, brother of assassinated president John F. Kennedy, announces that he will be running for the Democratic presidential nomination.

> **❝** *I am concerned about the whole man. I am concerned about what the people, using their government as an instrument and a tool, can do toward building the whole man, which will mean a better society and a better world.* **❞**
>
> Lyndon B. Johnson

Vietnam President Johnson announces a partial halt to bombing. General Westmoreland requests 206,000 more troops; he is later relieved of his command as a result of the Tet Offensive. At My Lai, under the command of Lieutenant William L. Calley Jr, 105 US troops massacre 504 Vietnamese villagers; Calley will be charged with six counts of premeditated murder and in 1971 is sentenced to life imprisonment with hard labour; a day after being passed, the sentence is commuted by President Richard Nixon to three and a half years' house arrest.

Indonesia General Suharto succeeds Sukarno as president of Indonesia; he thwarts a communist coup and assumes power; thousands of alleged communists are executed amid widespread violence.

Mauritius gains independence from Britain.

Maldives The ruling Sultanate is abolished and a republic is established.

Science & Technology: The Lockheed C-5A Galaxy, the biggest plane in the world, is demonstrated by the US Air Force.

Entertainment: Country singers Johnny Cash and June Carter marry.

Born: Damon Albarn, British musician (Blur). Mike Atherton, English cricketer. Daniel Craig, British actor. Céline Dion, Canadian singer.

Died: Yuri Gagarin, Russian cosmonaut, first man in space, aged 34.

April

United Kingdom Conservative politician Enoch Powell makes his anti-immigration 'Rivers of Blood' speech in Birmingham. London Bridge is sold to a US oil company; it is re-located to Arizona.

West Germany There are riots in West Berlin following the attempted assassination of student leader, Rudi Dutschke by a right-wing extremist, Josef Bachmann; Dutschke will die in 1980 from health problems related to the shooting. Andreas Baader and Gudrun Ensslin are convicted of arson after planting bombs in two department stores in Frankfurt-am-Main; Baader flees after sentencing and will be re-arrested in 1970. In elections in Baden-Wurttemberg, the far-right National Democratic Party gains 12 seats.

Czechoslovakia Alexander Dubček affirms his determination to make communism in Czechoslovakia more democratic.

Canada The charismatic Pierre Trudeau succeeds Lester Pearson as the country's 15th prime minister; he will remain Canada's prime minister until 1984 with a break of only nine months from June 1979 to March 1980.

USA Dr Martin Luther King is assassinated on the balcony of his room in the Lorraine Motel in Memphis by James Earl Ray; there is serious rioting in 125 American cities. 41 die in a double explosion in Richmond, Indiana. 16-year-old Black Panther Bobby Hutton is shot dead during a shootout between Panthers and Oakland police; Eldridge Cleaver is arrested. The bureau of narcotics and dangerous drugs, the Drug Enforcement Administration (DEA), is established.

Vietnam North Vietnam agrees to meet US representatives to discuss preliminary peace talks. The siege of Khe Sanh ends after 77 days; the Americans remain in control; more than 1,600 North Vietnamese troops are estimated to have died but thousands more are thought to have died in bombing. General Creighton Abrams replaces General Westmoreland. The Pentagon announces that troops will start to be withdrawn with more responsibility being given to the South Vietnamese army.

Sierra Leone A coup installs a new government under Siaka Stevens; he will rule a one-party state for 17 years.

New Zealand During Cyclone Giselle, New Zealand experiences its strongest ever winds; the ferry *Wahine* hits a reef at the entrance to Wellington Harbour and sinks with the loss of 53 lives.

• •

Entertainment: Stanley Kubrick's *2001: A Space Odyssey* premieres. The rock musical *Hair* premieres at the Biltmore Theatre on Broadway.

Sport: World Champion racing driver Jim Clark is killed during a Formula Two race at Hockenheim.

Born: Tony Hawk, US skateboarder. Timothy McVeigh, US terrorist.

Died: Dr Martin Luther King assassinated, age 39.

• •

May

United Kingdom London gangsters, the Kray twins, Ron and Reggie, and 16 associates are convicted of murder and sentenced to life imprisonment; they will not be eligible for parole for 30 years; their brother Charlie gets 10 years.

France Students and workers riot and strike in France, protesting against the government of de Gaulle and Pompidou; 1,000 are injured in Paris; the Paris Bourse is set on fire; many believe it to be the start of a revolution and the government is almost brought down.

Gibraltar Spain closes its frontier, allowing only Spaniards to cross.

Italy Following a general election, Christian Democrat Giovanni Leone retains his position as prime minister.

Czechoslovakia Alexander Dubček announces liberalizing reforms designed to give his country 'socialism with a human face'; he announces plans for freedom of the press, freedom of speech, and freedom of movement, with economic emphasis on consumer goods and the possibility of a multiparty government.

Nigeria Nigerian troops take Port Harcourt and encircle Biafra; a humanitarian disaster ensues as the Biafran population starves.

USA 99 sailors die when the nuclear-powered submarine *Scorpion* sinks 643 km (400 miles) south-west of the Azores.

Vietnam Preliminary peace talks begin in Paris.

• •

Entertainment: The Beatles announce the creation of their multimedia company Apple Corps Ltd.

Sport: On a night of high emotion, Manchester United become the first English club to win the European Cup when they beat Benfica of Portugal 4–1 in the final at Wembley. Jim 'Catfish' Hunter of the Oakland Athletics pitches the first perfect game in the American League for 47 years.

Born: Crown Prince Frederik of Denmark. Kylie Minogue, Australian actress and singer.

• •

June

United Nations The General Assembly adopts a treaty on the non-proliferation of nuclear weapons, effective in 1970.

United Kingdom James Earl Ray, fugitive killer of Martin Luther King, is apprehended in London. The government introduces charges for NHS prescriptions.

Spain The Basque separatist organization, ETA, kills for the first time when a policeman is shot dead at a checkpoint.

Italy Christian Democrat Giovanni Leone becomes prime minister for a second time.

Czechoslovakia Freedom of the press, assembly and religion and rehabilitation of political prisoners is announced.

Rhodesia The United Kingdom imposes sanctions.

Canada Pierre Trudeau's Liberal Party wins a big victory in the Federal elections.

USA Senator Robert Kennedy, campaigning for the Democratic Party's presidential nomination, is shot by Sirhan Sirhan in the Ambassador Hotel in Los Angeles; he dies in hospital the following day. Daniel Ellsberg is indicted for leaking the Pentagon Papers, top secret Department of Defense history of US political and military involvement in Vietnam from 1945 to 1967; they provide evidence that the government has long known that the war in Vietnam is unwinnable.

Uruguay President Areco imposes price and wage freezes in an attempt to control inflation; he enforces a state of emergency following labour disputes; constitutional safeguards are repealed and the government uses torture during interrogations, ruthlessly represses demonstrations, and imprisons all opponents; a group of students forms the Tupamaros revolutionary group and begins a campaign of urban guerrilla warfare, kidnapping and later releasing a number of foreign nationals, robbing banks, freeing political prisoners and assassinating police officials; martial law persists until March 1969.

Argentina 74 people are killed and more than 150 injured when fans stampede at a football stadium in Buenos Aires.

• •

Art: Andy Warhol is shot and wounded by radical feminist Valerie Solanas, founder of SCUM (the Society for Cutting Up Men).

Sport: In the replayed final of football's European Chamionship after the first match has ended in a draw, Italy beats Yugoslavia 2–0.

Born: Jason Donovan, Australian singer and actor.

Died: Dan Duryea, US actor, 60. Tony Hancock, British comedian, 44. Helen Keller, blind and deaf US author and lecturer, 87.

••

July

The World 16 nations sign a nuclear non-proliferation treaty.

Belgium Christian Democrat, Gaston Eyskens, is elected prime minister for the third time since 1949.

Vatican Pope Paul VI issues the encyclical *Humanae Vitae* reaffirming the Catholic Church's opposition to abortion and to all contraception except the rhythm method.

Israel and Egypt engage in an artillery duel along the Suez Canal.

Iraq The Arab Socialist Ba'ath Party stages a bloodless coup; General Ahmed Hassan al-Bakr becomes president; Saddam Hussein soon becomes recognized as the strongman of the regime, taking control of the country's internal security.

••

Entertainment: *Dad's Army*, a sitcom about the Home Guard in World War II is broadcast for the first time.

Science & Technology: Intel, the world's largest semiconductor company and the inventor of the x86 series of microprocessors, the processors found in most personal computers, is founded by Robert Noyce and Gordon Moore.

Sport: Alec Rose completes his 354-day circumnavigation of the world on his yacht *Lively Lady*; he is knighted the following day.

Born: Rhys Ifans, Welsh actor.

••

August

United Kingdom The last steam passenger train service runs. The first-ever issue of the listings magazine, *Time Out*, is published.

France becomes the world's fifth thermonuclear power when it explodes a hydrogen bomb in the South Pacific.

Norway Crown Prince Harald marries Sonja Haraldsen, a commoner.

Iceland Dr Kristján Eldjárn replaces Ásgeir Ásgeirsson as the country's third president.

Greece An assassination attempt on Prime Minister Colonel George Papadopoulos, organized by poet and politician Alexandros Panagoulis, fails; Panagoulis is arrested and sentenced to death but his sentence is commuted to imprisonment following pressure from the international community.

Vatican Pope Paul VI is the first pope to visit Latin America when he arrives in Bogota, Colombia.

Czechoslovakia The Bratislava Statement affirms the country's right to determine its own path; the USSR announces military manoeuvres along the Czech border; on 20 August, 650,000 troops of the Soviet Union and other Warsaw Pact countries invade and crush the 'Prague Spring' liberalization initiated by Alexander Dubček.

Iran 12,000 die in an earthquake.

USA Richard Nixon wins the Republican Party's nomination for president with Spiro Agnew as his running mate. Thousands of anti-Vietnam war demonstrators protest at the Democratic Party's convention in Chicago and 11,000 Chicago police, 6,000 National Guard, 7,500 troops, 1,000 FBI agents respond ruthlessly; Vice-President Hubert Humphrey is nominated on a platform supporting the war.

Japan 104 die when two charter buses plunge into the Hida River during torrential rain.

Vietnam There are now 541,000 US troops in the country.

Entertainment: Big Brother and the Holding Company, with Janis Joplin as lead singer, release their album *Cheap Thrills.* The Jimi Hendrix Experience's third and final album, *Electric Ladyland,* is released.

August 1968
Sport: Arthur Ashe becomes the first black tennis player to win the United States Tennis Championship. He set another record in 1968, which may never be equalled. He won both the US Amateur and the US Open championships, the first and only time such a double win has been accomplished.

Born: Gillian Anderson, US actress. Darren Clarke, Northern Irish Golfer. Colin McRae, British rally driver. Jason Leonard, British rugby player.
Died: Princess Marina, Duchess of Kent, 62.

September

United Kingdom France once again vetoes Britain's entry into the Common Market. Marlborough College becomes the first boys' public school to admit girls. A two-tier postal service is introduced; first class stamps cost fivepence, second class fourpence.

France 95 people die in a plane crash near Nice.

Portugal 79-year-old Portuguese dictator, António Salazar suffers a major stroke, after falling from a chair in his summer house; President Américo Thomaz replaces him with Professor Marcelo Caetano; Salazar has ruled dictatorially for 36 years and it is said that, until he dies in 1970, he thinks he is still in charge.

Albania withdraws from the Warsaw Pact in response to the invasion of Czechoslovakia.

Greece A referendum gives the ruling military junta more powers.

Republic of the Congo A military coup deposes President Alphonse Massamba-Débat; he is replaced by leftist Marien Ngouabi who, had been demoted for political reasons by Massamba-Débat from captain to ordinary soldier in 1966.

Nigeria The Organization of African Unity condemns the secession of Biafra.

Pakistan Hijackers kill 21 on board a Pan Am jet in Karachi.

Swaziland gains independence from Britain; Sobhuza II rules as king in an attempt at a constitutional monarchy; he has been paramount chief of the country since 1899 and his reign, ending with his death in 1982, at 82 years and 9 months, is the longest reign of any monarch since antiquity.

USA The Big Mac is created by Pittsburgh McDonald's franchisee, Jim Delligatti.

• •

Science & Technology: The first Boeing 747 is rolled out. The unmanned Russian spacecraft *Zond 5* becomes the first to loop around the Moon and return to Earth.

Sport: An MCC cricket tour of South Africa is cancelled when the South Africans refuse to accept Basil D'Oliveira, a cricketer of South African origin selected to play for the English side, who is classified by the apartheid system as 'coloured', and, therefore, not eligible to play first-class cricket.

Born: Mohamed Atta, Egyptian terrorist. Will Smith, US actor.

Died: Chester Carlson, US inventor of the photocopier, aged 62.

• •

October

United Kingdom Catholic demonstrators clash with police in Northern Ireland; The incident is considered to mark the beginning of 'the Troubles'. A massive anti-Vietnam War demonstration takes place in London.

Greece Greek shipping magnate, Aristotle Onassis, marries Jacqueline Kennedy, widow of assassinated President John F. Kennedy, on the island of Skorpios.

Democratic Republic of the Congo Rebel leader, Pierre Mulele, lured out of exile by President Mobutu who has promised him an amnesty, is executed after being horrifically tortured.

Equatorial Guinea receives its independence from Spain; Francisco Macías Nguema is elected president but establishes a one-party state and abrogates key parts of the constitution; he will rule until 1979.

Mexico Following months of unrest in Mexico, 300 demonstrating students are shot dead while others are arrested and beaten indiscriminately by police in Mexico City just ten days prior to the opening of the Olympic Games.

Panama The democratically elected President Arnulfo Arias is ousted in a military coup led by General Omar Torrijos; Torrijos never becomes president, but controls the country until 1981 as 'Maximum Leader of the Panamanian Revolution' and 'El Supremo Supremo'.

Peru The Belaunde government resigns over President Belaunde's decision to pay Standard Oil compensation for handing over their installation to Peru; Juan Velasco Alvarado seizes power in a 'military revolution'; he assumes the title of President of the Revolutionary Government of the Armed Forces; he nationalizes entire industries including fisheries, mining, telecommunications and power and will rule until 1975.

Jamaica Riots known as the Rodney Riots break out when Prime Minister Hugh Shearer's government bans black activist Guyanese university lecturer Dr Walter Rodney from returning to his teaching position at the University of the West Indies; several people die and millions of dollars of damage is caused.

Vietnam President Johnson announces a halt to all US bombing of North Vietnam.

• •

Entertainment: John Lennon and Yoko Ono are arrested on drugs offences. Led Zeppelin play their first-ever gig, at Surrey University.

Science & Technology: *Apollo 7*, the first manned Apollo mission, makes 163 orbits of the Earth; astronauts Wally Schirra, Donn Eisele, Walter Cunningham are on board; the *Apollo* series is designed to put a man on the Moon.

Sport: The Games of the 19th Olympiad are opened in Mexico City; 32 African nations decide to boycott the Games because of the presence of South Africa; US athletes, Tommy Smith and John Carlos make the Black Power salute during their victory ceremony; they are suspended by the US Olympic Committee.

The 'Fosbury Flop'

• •

The Fosbury Flop was a style of high jump popularized and perfected by American athlete Dick Fosbury, whose gold medal win in the 1968 Olympics in Mexico City, bought it to the world's attention. In his unusual 'flip-flop' style, Fosbury set an Olympic record as he cleared the bar in the high jump event at 2.2479 m (7 ft 4½ inches). Over the next few years, the flop became the dominant style of the event and remains so today. Before the Fosbury Flop, most jumpers used the Straddle technique, Western Roll, Eastern cut-off or even Scissors-Jump to clear the bar. Because the landing surfaces used to be either sandpits or low piles of matting, high jumpers of earlier years needed to land carefully to prevent injury. With the advent of deep foam matting, high jumpers were able to be more adventurous in their jumping styles, without having to land on their feet.

Born: Thom Yorke, British singer (Radiohead).

Died: Marcel Duchamp, French painter, 81. Ramon Navarro, Mexican actor, 69.

. . . .

November

Greece At the funeral of former prime minister, Georgios Papandreou, 300,000 demonstrate against the military junta ruling the country.

USA Richard Nixon defeats Hubert Humphrey and George Wallace in the presidential election. Yale University admits women students. Stewart Brand publishes *The Whole Earth Catalogue*, a counter-culture catalogue, described by Apple founder Steve Jobs as the conceptual forerunner of the World Wide Web.

. . . .

Born: Russell Jones, 'Ol' Dirty Bastard', US rapper (Wu-Tang Clan).

Died: Georgios Papandreou, former Greek prime minister, 80. Upton Sinclair, US author, 90.

. . . .

December

Italy Christian Democrat, Mariano Rumor, is elected prime minister.

Lebanon Israel attacks an airport in Beirut, destroying 13 planes.

Palestine Dr George Habash founds the Popular Front for the Liberation of Palestine (PFLP).

Mali becomes a police state when Moussa Traoré deposes President Modibo Keïta in a military coup; he becomes head of the Comité Militaire de Libération Nationale, effectively making him head of state and rules ruthlessly until 1991.

Republic of the Congo President Ngouabi changes the country's name to the People's Republic of the Congo and declares it to be Africa's first Marxist-Leninist state; he founds the Congolese Workers' Party as the country's only legal political party.

USA President Nixon names Henry Kissinger as his security advisor.

Brazil President Artur da Costa e Silva introduces the A-15 Act, giving him the power to dismiss the National Congress, strip politicians of their positions and bring in oppressive measures; it marks the beginning of harsh military rule that will last until 1978.

Japan The biggest robbery in Japanese history, the '300 Million Yen Robbery', takes place in Tokyo; a man disguised as a policeman steals the money when he fools bank officials into believing that there is a bomb in the car in which they are transporting the cash; no one is ever arrested and the money remains unrecovered.

Vietnam President Nixon announces a third round of troop withdrawals.

. . . .

Entertainment: Crosby, Stills & Nash appear together for the first time. The Beatles release *The White Album*.

Science & Technology: *Apollo 8*, with astronauts, Borman, Lovell and Anders, makes the first manned orbit of the Moon; they are the first humans to leave the influence of Earth's gravity and orbit another world.

Died: Tallulah Bankhead, US actress, 66. Trygve Lie, Norwegian first United Nations Secretary General, 72. John Steinbeck, US author, 66.

. . . .

Highlights of 1968

MAJOR FILMS

*2001: A Space
    Odyssey*
Bullitt
*Chitty Chitty Bang
    Bang*
Funny Girl
Ice Station Zebra
*Night of the Living
    Dead*
*Once Upon a Time
    in the West*
Planet of the Apes
The Odd Couple
The Producers

Roddy McDowell (Cornelius), Kim Hunter (Zira) and Charlton Heston
(George Taylor) in *Planet of the Apes* directed by
Franklin J. Schaffner

HIT RECORDS

All Along The Watchtower Jimi Hendrix Experience
Born To Be Wild Steppenwolf
Delilah Tom Jones
Hello, I Love You The Doors
Hey Jude The Beatles
I Heard It Through The Grapevine Marvin Gaye
Jumpin' Jack Flash Rolling Stones
Mrs. Robinson Simon & Garfunkel
(Sittin' On The) Dock Of The Bay Otis Redding
What a Wonderful World Louis Armstrong

BEST-SELLING BOOKS

A Kestrel for a Knave Barry Hines
Chariots of the Gods: Unsolved Mysteries of the Past Erik
    von Daniken
Airport Arthur Hailey
The Armies of the Night Norman Mailer
The Electric Kool-Aid Acid Test Tom Wolfe
The Teachings of Don Juan Carlos Castaneda

GIANT LEAP
FOR MANKIND

1969

January

United Kingdom Australian media baron, Rupert Murdoch buys Britain's biggest-selling newspaper, the *News of the World*. In Northern Ireland, a march takes place from Belfast to Derry in support of civil rights; the Royal Ulster Constabulary (RUC) assault inhabitants and damage property in the Bogside area of Derry; residents build barricades and establish the self-autonomous nationalist area of Free Derry. Hardline Northern Ireland Protestant leader, Reverend Ian Paisley, is jailed for three months for illegal assembly. Violent protests by students at the London School of Economics close it for three weeks. Sir Leary Constantine, West Indian cricketer and statesman, becomes Britain's first black peer. The Open University is founded.

Spain There is a wave of strikes and protests across Spain; martial law is declared in response to rioting in Madrid in which 300 students are arrested.

Czechoslovakia Student Jan Palach becomes a martyr when he sets himself on fire in Prague's Wenceslas Square in protest at the Soviet invasion; he dies three days later.

Morocco Spain returns the Ifni province to Morocco.

Iraq 14 men, nine of them Jews, are publicly executed in Baghdad for allegedly spying for Israel.

USA Richard Nixon is sworn in as 37th president of the United States.

Vietnam Peace talks resume in Paris.

••

Entertainment: *Led Zeppelin 1*, one of the very first heavy metal albums, is released to critical acclaim. Police break up the last public performance by the Beatles on the roof of their Apple offices in Saville Row; the performance will feature in their film, *Let It Be*.

Science & Technology: When Russian-manned spacecraft dock in orbit, Yevgeny Khrunov becomes the first man to transfer between linked capsules. NASA unveils its moon-landing craft.

Born: Dave Grohl, US drummer and singer (Nirvana, Foo Fighters). Stephen Hendry, Scottish snooker player. Roy Jones Jr, US boxer. Marilyn Manson, US singer. Michael Schumacher, German racing driver.

Died: Meher Baba, Indian mystic and spiritual master, 74. Allan Welsh Dulles, US diplomat and former director of the CIA, 75.

••

February

Palestine At the Palestinian National Congress in Cairo, Yasser Arafat, leader of Al-Fatah, becomes leader of the Palestine Liberation Organization (PLO); members of the PLO machine-gun an El-Al plane in Zurich in Switzerland.

Canada The Front de Libération du Québec bombs the Montreal Stock Exchange; many are injured and a huge amount of damage is caused.

USA The population reaches 200 million. The last issue of the *Saturday Evening Post* goes on sale; it closes after being published for 147 years. Student protests about the Vietnam War continue across America.

Vietnam President Nixon approves the secret bombing of Cambodia; thousands of students demonstrate when Nixon visits Rome and West Berlin.

••

Science & Technology: The Boeing 747, the world's largest passenger plane, makes its maiden flight.

Born: Jennifer Aniston, US actress. Retief Goosen, South African golfer.

Died: Levi Eshkol, Israeli prime minister, 73. Gabby Hayes, US actor, 83.

Karl Jaspers, German psychiatrist and philosopher, 86. Boris Karloff, British actor, 81. King Saud of Saudi Arabia, 67.

March

United Kingdom Eight people die when the *Longhope* lifeboat from Orkney sinks.

West Germany Gustav Heinemann succeeds Heinrich Lübke as president.

USSR and China Many die in skirmishes at a border outpost on the Ussuri River.

Israel Golda Meir becomes the fourth prime minister of Israel and its first female leader.

USA James Earl Ray pleads guilty to the murder of Dr Martin Luther King and is sentenced to 99 years; he later withdraws his guilty plea. In a court in Los Angeles, Sirhan Sirhan admits to assassinating Robert Kennedy.

Venezuela Rafael Caldera succeeds Raúl Leoni as president; it is the first time in Venezuela's 139 years of independence that an incumbent government has peacefully surrendered power to an elected member of the opposition.

Vietnam There are now 543,000 US troops in Vietnam. President Nixon predicts he will end the war in 1970. The USA launches Operation Breakfast, the covert bombing of Cambodia.

OPERATION BREAKFAST

On 9 February 1969, US military intelligence reported that there was a significant North Vietnamese army base just inside Cambodia. General Creighton Abrahms, commander of the US forces in Vietnam, was confident that a series of precision B-52 bomber strikes would be enough to eliminate the base, assuming, of course, that he could convince the new Nixon administration to go along with his plan. B-52s were one of the most lethal non-nuclear forms of attack, as they could be used to cover large areas of land. The idea was pitched to Nixon, who didn't hesitate in approving the bombing with the assistance of his national security advisor Henry Kissinger. The first airstrikes were set for March, barely one month after the initial intelligence reports. In honour of the breakfast meeting held at the Pentagon that led to Nixon's approval of the strike, the assault was aptly codenamed 'Operation Breakfast'. However, despite months of airstrikes, the bombings did little to curb NVA activities. On the contrary, communist forces crept further and further into Cambodia.

Anguilla A contingent of British 'Red Devil' Brigade paratroops, plus 40 London police officers, land on the Caribbean island, part of a British dependency, following two rebellions and a brief period as a self-proclaimed independent republic under the leadership of Ronald Webster, who has been ruling as president since 1967; British rule is re-established.

Entertainment: Jim Morrison, lead singer of The Doors, is arrested for exposing himself onstage in Miami. Paul McCartney marries Linda Eastman; John Lennon marries Yoko Ono and the couple embark on a 'bed-in' for peace in Amsterdam. The *Smothers Brothers'* television show is cancelled in America for being too controversial.

Science & Technology: Concorde undergoes its first test flight. In Earth's orbit, astronauts Jim McDivitt, Dave Scott and Rusty Schweickart on the *Apollo 9* space mission perform the first manned flight of the lunar landing module, the first docking and extraction of the lunar module and the first docking of two manned spacecraft; the mission proves the lunar module worthy of manned spaceflight.

Sport: Mickey Mantle of the New York Yankees announces his retirement from baseball.

Born: Javier Bardem, Spanish actor.

Died: Dwight D. Eisenhower, former US president and World War II general, 79. Frank Loesser, US songwriter, 59. John Kennedy Toole, US author, 32. B Traven, US author, 79. John Wyndham, British author, 65.

❝ *Every gun that is made, every warship launched, every rocket fired, signifies in the final sense a theft from those who hunger and are not fed, those who are cold and are not clothed.* ❞

Dwight D. Eisenhower

April

United Kingdom British troops are sent to Northern Ireland to support the Royal Ulster Constabulary.

France President Charles de Gaulle resigns following the defeat of his plans to reform the Senate, the upper house of the French Parliament, into an advisory body, while extending more powers to regional councils; it is suggested that de Gaulle is merely committing political suicide after the traumatic events of 1968.

Spain Basque separatist violence continues as Fermín Monasterio Pérez is killed by ETA in Biscay; he is their fourth victim.

Czechoslovakia Alexander Dubček is removed from power; the 'Prague Spring' is over.

Palestine The Palestinians battle with Lebanese troops.

USA Sirhan Sirhan is sentenced to death for assassinating Robert Kennedy; the sentence is later commuted to life imprisonment.

Bolivia Three-time president, General René Barrientos is killed in a helicopter crash; Luis Adolfo Siles Salinas succeeds him.

China Lin Biao is named as Chairman Mao Zedong's successor in sweeping changes to the leadership of the Chinese Communist Party.

North Korea There is an international incident when North Korean guns shoot down an EC-121 reconnaissance plane over the Sea of Japan, killing all 31 crew members.

Vietnam US B-52s drop 3000-ton bombs on the Cambodian border. US troop numbers in Vietnam peak at 543,000; more than 33,000 have died in the conflict, more than in the Korean War.

· ·

Entertainment: Beatle Paul McCartney denies rumours that he has died.

Medicine & Health: The first artificial heart is implanted by Dr Denton Cooley; it has been designed by Dr Domingo Liotta. The first human eye transplant is carried out.

Science & Technology: The Hawker Siddeley Harrier enters service with the RAF; it is the only successful vertical/short take-off and landing plane.

April 1969
Sport: British polar explorer, Wally Herbert, becomes the first man to cross the frozen surface 5,976 km (3,720 miles) of the Arctic Ocean on foot. From Front row (l–r): Wally Herbert, team leader, Major Kenneth Heges, medical officer. Back row: Squad leader Freddie Church, who was stationed in Northern Canada acting as radio operator, Alan Gill and Dr Roy Koerner, the team's glaciologist. It took 16 months to complete the journey.

Sport: British yachtsman, Robin Knox-Johnstone, becomes the first man to make a single-handed non-stop circumnavigation of the globe.

Born: Renée Zelleweger, US actress.

Died: General René Barrientos, president of Bolivia, 50. Helena Rubenstein, US cosmetics manufacturer, 89.

May

United Kingdom The voting age is reduced to 18.

Democratic Republic of the Congo Paratroopers of the French Foreign Legion land in Kolwezi, to rescue Europeans in the middle of fighting taking place in the country.

Sudan Following a series of unsatisfactory governments, Colonel Gaafar al-Nimeiry, stages a coup and becomes prime minister; the new regime abolishes parliament and outlaws all political parties.

Canada Abortion and contraception are legalized.

Argentina Strikes and demonstrations break out in protest at injustices under the dictatorial rule of de facto president, General Juan Carlos Ongania. On 21 May there is a silent protest march in the city of Rosario in which a 15-year-old boy is killed by police; Rosario is declared an emergency zone under military jurisdiction and 7,000 people attend the funeral; strikes and demonstrations continue; the protest movement becomes known as the Rosariazo.

Curaçao Large-scale rioting signals the start of an Afro-Caribbean civil rights movement on the island; the civil unrest fuels a social movement that results in the local Afro-Caribbean population gaining more influence over the political process.

Vietnam The Battle of Dong Ap Bia, also known as Hamburger Hill, begins; following heavy casualties, US troops finally take the hill on 20 May.

Malaysia Following its third general election since independence, tensions between Malays and Chinese erupt in bloody riots; dozens die.

Entertainment: The Monty Python comedy group is formed when Graham Chapman, John Cleese, Terry Gilliam, Eric Idle, Terry Jones and Michael Palin get together to write and record a sketch show for BBC television. The Who release their rock opera, *Tommy*. Construction of Walt Disney World begins in Florida. John Lennon and Yoko Ono record *Give Peace a Chance* while conducting a bed-in for peace in the Queen Elizabeth Hotel in Montreal in Canada; it marks the first solo outing by the Beatle and is released under the name the Plastic Ono Band; it remains an anthem for peace that is sung to this day.

Science & Technology: *Apollo 10*'s manned lunar module flies to within 14.4 km (9 miles) of the surface of the Moon; astronauts Thomas P. Stafford, John W. Young and Eugene A. Cernan are on board. The Soviet space probe, *Venera 5*, lands on Venus.

Born: Dennis Bergkamp, Dutch footballer. Cate Blanchett, Australian actress. Brian Lara, West Indian cricketer.

Died: Franz von Pappen, former German Chancellor, 89. Osbert Sitwell, British poet, 76.

June

United Kingdom High-grade crude oil is discovered in the North Sea.

France Georges Pompidou, former prime minister, succeeds Charles de Gaulle as president.

USSR Russian and Chinese troops clash on the Sinkiang border. The

International Meeting of Communist and Workers Parties is held in Moscow; it is the first such meeting since 1960 and occurs in the aftermath of the Sino-Soviet split and the Russian invasion of Czechoslovakia.

Nigeria The Nigerian government bans all Red Cross aid to Biafra; two weeks later it allows medical supplies in, but still prohibits food.

Rhodesia The United Kingdom severs diplomatic ties.

Canada Tobacco advertising is banned on radio and television.

USA Black Panther William Brent is the 28th person to hijack an American plane to Cuba. The gay rights movement begins when patrons of the Stonewall Bar in New York's Greenwich Village clash with police; the riots continue for three days. 74 US sailors are killed when the Australian aircraft carrier *Melbourne* collides with the US destroyer, *Frank E. Evans,* in the South China Sea. The National Convention of Students for a Democratic Society in Chicago collapses when it is hijacked by the radical left Weatherman faction.

Honduras and El Salvador sever diplomatic ties with each other following riots during a World Cup match; tens of thousands of Salvadorian workers are expelled from Honduras prompting El Salvador to briefly invade and the two countries fight a four-day war known as the Football War; a cease-fire takes effect on 20 July.

Vietnam President Nixon meets South Vietnamese president, Thieu, and tells him that 25,000 US troops will be withdrawn by August.

• •

Entertainment: The last episode of *Star Trek* is shown on television. The musical *Oh Calcutta!* Opens in New York. Captain Beefheart and his Magic Band release the avant garde album *Trout Mask Replica.*

Born: Steffi Graf, German tennis player. Oliver Kahn, German footballer. Paul Tergat, Kenyan athlete.

Died: Judy Garland, US singer and actress, 47.

• •

July

United Kingdom Prince Charles is invested as Prince of Wales, customary title of the heir to the British throne.

July 1969

United Kingdom: After 700 years, the halfpenny ceases to be legal tender. This coin was not usually called a 'half penny', nor was the plural usually said as 'half pence'. The usual pronunciation was 'hayp-knee' referring to a single coin (with subtle variations depending on where in England you lived), or 'hay-punce' in the plural as in 'three halfpence'. The first halfpennies were literally pennies cut in half and for several centuries, silver pennies were the only coins produced. It wasn't until the reign of Charles II in 1672, that copper halfpennies were issued for the first time.

Kenya Tom Mboya, minister of development and a key figure in the founding of the ruling party, the Kenyan African Union (KANU), is assassinated; the tribal elite around President Jomo Kenyatta, believing Mboya to be a threat to Kenyatta, has been blamed for his death.

Canada The French language is made equal to English throughout the government.

USA A scandal erupts when a car driven by Senator Edward Kennedy plunges from a bridge on Chappaquiddick Island, near Martha's Vineyard; his passenger, Mary Jo Kopechne drowns; Kennedy is charged with leaving the scene of an accident. President Nixon explains the 'Nixon Doctrine' that America's Asian allies will be expected to take care of their own military defence.

Vietnam US troop withdrawals begin.

FIRST MAN ON THE MOON

20 July 1969 was an epic day in life of *Apollo 11* astronaut, Neil Armstrong, as he became the first man ever to take steps on the Moon. He stepped out of the spacecraft at 0256 GMT, nearly 20 minutes after first opening the hatch on the *Eagle* landing craft. He had earlier reported back to Houston with the words: 'Houston, Tranquility Base here. The *Eagle* has landed.' His first steps were in the Sea of Tranquility and he described the surface as being like powdered charcoal. As he placed his left foot down onto the surface of the Moon, Armstrong proudly declared: 'That's one small step for man, one giant leap for mankind'. When the lunar module landed on the surface, it left craters about 0.3 m (1 ft) deep and the historic moments were captured on television cameras which were installed on the *Eagle* and turned on by Armstrong himself. The world looked on in amazement as Armstrong, joined by his colleague Edwin 'Buzz' Aldrin, jumped across the surface of the Moon before planting the Stars and Stripes flag at 0341 GMT.

Entertainment: Brian Jones, former guitarist for the Rolling Stones, drowns in a swimming pool at his house. The film *Easy Rider,* starring Peter Fonda and Dennis Hopper, premieres. The supergroup Blind Faith is formed; members are guitarists Eric Clapton, keyboard player and singer Stevie Winwood and drummer Ginger Baker.

Sport: The trimaran of English yachtsman, Donald Crowhurst, a competitor in the *Sunday Times* Golden Globe Round the World Yacht Race is found adrift in the North Atlantic; Crowhurst had been thought to be winning the race, but it emerges that he has not actually circumnavigated the Earth; he is believed to have lost his mind and committed suicide by jumping overboard.

Born: Tanni Grey-Thompson, British Paralympian. Jennifer Lopez, US singer.

Died: Otto Dix, German artist, 78. Walter Gropius, German architect and founder of the Bauhaus school of design, 86. Brian Jones, former guitarist of the Rolling Stones, 27.

August

United Kingdom The Battle of the Bogside; three days of serious rioting breaks out in the Bogside area of Londonderry in Northern Ireland after a parade by the Protestant Apprentice Boys; the Troubles begin; British troops are sent to preserve peace but the Provisional IRA launches a campaign of bombs and violence.

USSR and China There are further, serious border clashes between troops of the two neighbours.

USA Sharon Tate, actress and pregnant wife of film director, Roman Polanski, is murdered along with four others by Charles Manson's cult the 'Family'. The next night, members of his 'Family' murder wealthy Los Angeles business-people, Leno and Rosemary LaBianca in their home. Hurricane Camille, a Category 5 hurricane and the most powerful tropical cyclonic system at landfall in recorded history, strikes the Mississippi coast; 248 die and damage worth $1.5 billion is caused. The FBI reports a 98 per cent increase in marijuana arrests compared to 1966.

Vietnam US Secretary of State, Henry Kissinger, begins secret peace talks with North Vietnamese representative, Xuan Thuy, in the apartment of French intermediary, Jean Sainteny, in Paris; neither side can agree on terms and they fail.

Entertainment: The Woodstock Music and Art Fair attracts 400,000 people to upstate New York to hear three days of music from, amongst others, Joan Baez, Jimi Hendrix, Crosby, Stills and Nash, Creedence Clearwater Revival, the Grateful Dead, Janis Joplin and Canned Heat.

Science & Technology: US space probe, *Mariner 7,* flies close to Mars.

Born: Jack Black, US actor and musician. Matthew Perry, Canadian actor.

Died: Theodor Adorno, German philosopher, 65. Ivy Compton-Burnett, British author, 85. Rocky Marciano, US boxing world champion, 45. Leonard Woolf, British author and publisher, 89.

September

United Kingdom Police raid a 100-room mansion at 144 Piccadilly which was being used as a squat by the so-called London Street Commune. The movement was formed in 1968 in response to the growing concern over homelessness.

West Germany The Social Democrats and the Free Democrats receive a majority of votes in parliamentary elections; they decide to form a coalition government.

Switzerland The males of the Swiss canton of Schaffhausen vote to reject female suffrage.

Libya A bloodless coup led by 27-year-old Muammar al-Gaddafi overthrows King Idris while he is in Greece receiving medical treatment; the monarchy is abolished and the new Libyan Arab Republic is proclaimed; Gaddafi reuses to promote himself to the rank of general, becoming a colonel instead; he claims that Libya's society is 'ruled by the people', so he requires no grander title or higher military rank.

USA The trial begins of the Chicago Eight (later Seven) who were arrested for staging demonstrations against the Vietnam War at the Democratic party Convention in 1968; five are convicted but the convictions are later overturned.

Bolivia General Alfredo Ovando Candia deposes President Siles in a coup to become dictator.

Vietnam President Nixon orders the resumption of the bombing of North Vietnam. North Vietnamese leader Ho Chi Minh dies of heart failure; he is not replaced as president, but a 'collective leadership' of ministers and military leaders takes control of North Vietnam.

· ·

Entertainment: John Lennon and the Plastic Ono band perform at the Toronto Peace Festival, Lennon's first live appearance in four years. The Beatles' last album, *Abbey Road*, is released.

Born: Shane Warne, Australian cricketer. Catherine Zeta-Jones, Welsh actress.

· ·

October

West Germany Social Democrat Party leader and former Mayor of West Berlin, Willi Brandt, becomes chancellor, succeeding Kurt Georg Kiesinger.

Sweden Olof Palme is elected Social Democrat Party leader and prime minister, replacing Tage Erlander who has been in power since 1946; Erlander holds the record – 23 years – for the longest-serving head of government of any democratic country.

USSR Dissident Soviet writer, Alexander Solzhenitsyn is expelled from the Soviet Writers' Union.

Morocco Ahmed Laraki becomes prime minister, succeeding Mohamed Benhima.

Nigeria Biafran leader General Ojukwu appeals to the United Nations to mediate a cease-fire in the conflict with Nigeria over its secession; the federal government calls for complete surrender.

Somalia Marxist General Mohamed Siad Barre stages a coup, six days after the assassination of President Abdirashid Ali Shermarke; Prime Minister Mohamed Ibrahim Egal is arrested and spends the next 12 years in prison.

USA Hundreds of thousands of people take part in National Moratorium peace protests across the country, including a candle-lit march around the White House; President Nixon addresses the nation on television and radio about the Vietnam War, asking the 'silent majority' to join him in solidarity with the war effort, and asking for support for his policies. The Days of Rage riots break out in Chicago where the National Guard is called in to control violent demonstrations involving the radical group, the Weathermen, protesting at the trial of the Chicago Eight. The

US Supreme Court orders immediate nationwide desegregation; race riots continue, however.

Brazil President Costa e Silva becomes ill and is replaced by Emílio Garrastazu Médici; he will rule for five years and if anything, will be even more repressive than the previous regime; there is torture and strict censorship of the press.

••

Entertainment: *Monty Python's Flying Circus* is shown on British television for the first time. The children's educational television show, *Sesame Street*, premieres on US television. Detroit band the MC5 record their influential album, *Kick Out the Jams,* live at the city's Grande Ballroom over two nights.

Science & Technology: Concorde breaks the sound barrier during a test flight. The first email message is sent by researchers at Stanford University using the US Department of Defence's Advanced Research and Projects Agency (ARPANET); ARPANET is the forerunner of the Internet.

Born: Ernie Els, South African golfer. Gwen Stefani, US singer.

Died: Jack Kerouac, US author, 47.

••

November

United Kingdom Regular colour television broadcasts begin on BBC1 and ITV.

USSR and USA begin the SALT 1 (Strategic Arms Limitations Treaties) negotiations in Helsinki to limit the number of nuclear weapons on each side.

Palestine A deal brokered by the Arab League gives the PLO refugee camps freedom from government interference.

USA A quarter of a million people protest peacefully against the Vietnam War in Washington.

Japan US President Nixon and Japanese prime minister, Eisaku Sato, agree that Okinawa will be returned to Japanese control in 1972; it has been used as a US military base since World War II.

November 1969
Vietnam: Explicit photographs of villagers killed in the My Lai massacre are published.

Entertainment: John Lennon returns his MBE in protest at the UK's involvement in the conflict in Biafra and at his record *Cold Turkey* slipping down the charts.

Science & Technology: *Apollo 12* astronauts, Charles Conrad and Alan Bean, spend 31 hours on the Moon. Scientists at Harvard isolate a single gene.

Sport: Brazilian soccer legend, Pele, scores his 1,000th goal.

Born: Sean 'P. Diddy' Combs, US rapper.

Died: Joseph P. Kennedy, financier and diplomat, father of President John F. Kennedy and Robert Kennedy, 81. Liu Shaoqi, former Chinese president, 71.

December

United Kingdom The Provisional Irish Republican Army (IRA) is founded in Northern Ireland.

Italy 17 die when a bomb explodes at the headquarters of *Banca Nazionale dell'Agricoltura* in Piazza Fontana, Milan; on the same day, three more bombs explode in Milan and Rome; the attacks are aimed to force the Italian state to proclaim a state of emergency in the face of a presumed communist insurgency; it is thought the bombs are the work of a far-right organization, Ordino Nuove.

Nigeria Biafra is cut in half by the Nigerian army; Ojukwu flees to the Ivory Coast; his chief-of-staff, Philip Effiong, is left in charge and will submit to the government in January 1970; more than a million people have died in battle or from hunger.

USA For the first time since World War II a draft lottery is held to determine the order of induction into the United States Army. Black Panther Party members Fred Hampton and Mark Clark are shot dead in their sleep during a raid by 14 Chicago police officers; officers involved in the shootings are cleared of any blame by a Grand Jury. LSD guru, Timothy Leary, is arrested for possession of marijuana and sentenced to 10 years in prison; he escapes in 1971 and remains free for several years before being recaptured.

Panama Demetrio B. Lakas becomes president; he has been chairman of the Provisional Junta of Government.

The World The population of the world is more than 3.5 billion.

Entertainment: The Rolling Stones play the Altamont Speedway in California in front of 300,000; Hell's Angels disrupt the show, murdering Meredith Hunter in front of the stage; Altamont is viewed as bringing the hedonistic 1960s to a close.

Born: Richard Hammond, British television presenter and motoring journalist. Jay-Z, US rapper.

Died: Princess Alice of Battenberg, mother of Prince Philip, Duke of Edinburgh, 84. Kliment Voroshilov, former president of the Soviet Union, 88.

MAJOR FILMS

*Butch Cassidy and the
    Sundance Kid*
Easy Rider
Kes
Midnight Cowboy
*On Her Majesty's Secret
    Service*
Paint Your Wagon
The Italian Job
*The Prime of Miss Jean
    Brodie*
The Wild Bunch
Women in Love

Dennis Hopper (Billy) from
Easy Rider, directed by
Dennis Hopper

HIT RECORDS

Aquarius/Let The Sunshine In The 5th Dimension
Get Back The Beatles
Honky Tonk Women The Rolling Stones
Albatross Fleetwood Mac
Je T'Aime, Moi Non Plus Serge Gainsburg and Jane Birkin
My Cherie Amour Stevie Wonder
My Way Frank Sinatra
Pinball Wizard The Who
Proud Mary Creedence Clearwater Revival
Whole Lotta Love Led Zeppelin

BEST-SELLING BOOKS

Delta of Venus Anaïs Nin
I Know Why the Caged Bird Sings Maya Angelou
I Sing the Body Electric Ray Bradbury
Inside the Third Reich Albert Speer
The Human Zoo Desmond Morris
The Very Hungry Caterpillar Eric Carle

THE BEATLES TIMELINE

1960

May The Quarry Men change their name to the Silver Beetles.

June First professional appearance at Neston Institute.

August Pete Best becomes the Silver Beetles' drummer. The band's line-up is John Lennon, Paul McCartney, George Harrison, Pete Best and Stuart Sutcliffe. They travel to Hamburg, Germany. The band's name is changed from the Silver Beetles to the Beatles and they perform for the first time with their new name at the Indra Club in Hamburg.

1961

February Lunchtime debut at the Cavern club.

March First night-time appearance at the Cavern club; paid £42. The band return to Hamburg.

June Perform as backing group for Tony Sheridan in recording studio.

July Stuart Sutcliffe remains in Hamburg when the band returns home.

October Brian Epstein, owner of the NEMS record shop in Liverpool, first hears about the Beatles when customer Raymond Jones asks in the shop for *My Bonnie* – the record they made in Hamburg with Tony Sheridan.

December Epstein becomes the Beatles' manager.

1962

January Fail an audition for Decca Records; A&R man Dick Rowe famously says, 'We don't like their sound. Groups of guitars are on the way out.'

March First radio appearance on the BBC Light Programme's *Teenager's Turn*.

April 1962
Former bass guitarist often referred to as the 'fifth Beatle', Stuart Sutcliffe, dies of a brain haemorrhage. He played with the Beatles for eighteen months and was the first bass player the Beatles ever had. It was his girlfriend who came up with the famous Beatle haircut that made history. Stuart Sutcliffe was just 22 when he died.

June The Fab Four sign a record deal with Parlophone / E.M.I. Audition for music producer George Martin at Abbey Road Studios.

August Pete Best is sacked; Ringo Starr joins as new drummer. John Lennon marries Cynthia Powell.

October *Love Me Do/PS I Love You* is released as a single in the UK, reaching number 17 in the *Melody Maker* singles chart. First TV performance, on Granada TV's *People and Places*.

December Return to Hamburg, for the last time.

1963

January *Please Please Me* is released, reaching number 2 in UK charts.

February British tour begins with Helen Shapiro bill-topping.

March The first Beatles album, *Please Please Me* is released in the UK.

April *From Me to You* is released and is the Beatles' first UK number 1.

August Last appearance at the Cavern. *She Loves You* is released, reaching number 1 in the UK.

November At the Royal Variety Performance John Lennon famously says to the audience: 'Those of you in the cheaper seats, clap your hands; and those of you in the more expensive seats, just rattle your jewellery.' The album, *With the Beatles* is released in Britain with 700,000 advance orders. *I Want To Hold Your Hand* is released, reaching number 1 in the UK.

1964

January *I Want To Hold Your Hand* becomes the Beatles' first US number 1, staying there for seven weeks and selling 2,000,000 copies.

February Welcomed by 3,000 screaming fans at Kennedy Airport. Perform on the Ed Sullivan Show, watched by 73 million.

March Begin filming their first movie, *A Hard Day's Night*. The *Meet The Beatles* album has sold 3,600,000 copies. The next single *Can't Buy Me Love* has advance orders of 1,700,000 copies in the USA and 1,000,000 in the UK. John Lennon's first book, *In His Own Write* is published.

April Beatles singles occupy the top five positions in the US charts.

June The album *A Hard Day's Night* is released.

July The film, *A Hard Day's Night*, is premiered in Liverpool. 100,000 line the streets.

November The single *I Feel Fine* is released.

1965

February Ringo Starr marries hairdresser Maureen Cox. Filming begins in the Bahamas for their second film, *Help!*

April The *Ticket to Ride* single is released.

June John Lennon's second book, *A Spaniard In the Works* is published.

July The *Help!* single is released.

August The *Help!* album and film are released. 56,000 watch the Beatles at Shea Stadium, New York, the largest rock concert attendance to date.

October Receive the MBE from the Queen.

December The *Rubber Soul* album is released. The *We Can Work it Out/Day Tripper* double A-side single is released.

1966

January George Harrison marries Pattie Boyd.

March John Lennon tells a journalist 'We're more popular than Jesus now'; four months later, the Ku Klux Klan and the southern Bible belt in the USA would denounce his claim and Beatles records would be temporarily banned around the world.

May The *Paperback Writer* single is released.

August The album *Revolver* is released. John Lennon apologizes for his Jesus remark. Last live performance in the US at San Francisco's Candlestick Park.

September John Lennon starts filming *How I Won the War*. George Harrison goes to India to study sitar with Ravi Shankar.

November John Lennon meets Yoko Ono for the first time at an exhibition of her art at the Indica Gallery in London. Recording of *Sergeant Pepper's Lonely Hearts Club Band* begins.

1967

February The *Strawberry Fields/Penny Lane* double A-side is released.

May EMI announces total world sales of Beatle records have reached 200 million. Paul McCartney meets Linda Eastman. The BBC bans *A Day in the Life from Sergeant Pepper* because – they claim – it contains drug references.

June *Sergeant Pepper's Lonely Hearts Club Band* is released to worldwide acclaim. Paul McCartney announces he has taken LSD four times. A televised performance of *All You Need Is Love* is seen live by satellite by 400 million viewers in 24 different countries; it is the first global satellite broadcast.

August The Beatles go to Bangor, North Wales for meditation with the Maharishi Mahesh Yogi. Brian Epstein dies of an overdose of sleeping pills.

October The *Hello Goodbye/I Am the Walrus* single is released.

November The *Magical Mystery Tour* EP is released.

December The Beatles' Apple Boutique opens in London. The *Magical Mystery Tour* television film airs in the UK only; reviews are universally poor and it is not shown in America.

1968

February John and George travel to Rishikesh, India, followed four days later by Paul and Ringo, for more meditation with the Maharishi.

March The *Lady Madonna* single is released. May Apple Corps, the Beatles' own company, is launched. Recording of *The Beatles* – popularly known as *The White Album* – begins.

July The animated film *Yellow Submarine* is premiered. The Apple Boutique fails; the stock is given away.

August Apple Records' first hit is released – Mary Hopkins' *Those Were the Days*. Ringo Starr walks out on the Beatles during recording of *The White Album*; he returns on 3 September. *Hey Jude* is released, selling 6 million copies worldwide.

September The Beatles perform *Hey Jude* on the David Frost TV show in the UK. ATV buys almost 50 per cent of Northern Songs, the Beatles' publishing company.

October John & Yoko are charged with possession of cannabis.

November Cynthia Lennon is granted a divorce from John. John and Yoko's *Unfinished Music No. 1: Two Virgins* is released. *The White Album* is released.

December The film *Candy*, starring Ringo Starr, Richard Burton and Marlon Brando is released.

After Paul McCartney's song *Penny Lane* became a big hit for the Beatles, the street signs for the actual Penny Lane in Liverpool disappeared with such regularity (as they did on the real Abbey Road), that the town reverted to simply painting the name on the buildings, rather than having street signs.

1969

January Filming of *Let It Be* begins. George Harrison walks out during recording, returning a week later. John Lennon announces that Apple Records is in financial chaos, saying, 'If it carries on like this, we'll be broke in six months.' The group makes its last live public appearance on the roof of the Apple building at 3 Savile Row.

February Allen Klein is appointed to look after the Beatles' affairs but Paul McCartney had wanted the job to go to Lee Eastman, his future wife Linda's father.

March George & Pattie Harrison's home is raided and they are fined for possession of cannabis. Paul McCartney marries Linda Eastman. John and Yoko marry in Gibraltar, following which they stage their first 'bed-in' for peace in room 902 at the Amsterdam Hilton.

April John and Yoko appear in a bag in Vienna.

May John and Yoko stage a 'bed-in' at Hotel La Reine Elizabeth, in Montreal.

June John and Yoko record *Give Peace A Chance* in their hotel room; it will be Lennon's first solo record. The Beatles' single *The Ballad of John and Yoko* is released.

July Recording of the *Abbey Road* album begins. *Give Peace A Chance* is released by the Plastic Ono Band.

August On 20 August, the Beatles record together for the last time.

September The 'Paul is dead' rumour sweeps the United States. John Lennon announces to the others that he is leaving the group.

October The *Abbey Road* album is released. The Plastic Ono Band release the single *Cold Turkey*.

November John Lennon returns his MBE to the Queen as a protest against British involvement in the conflict in Biafra and allegedly because *Cold Turkey* is sliding down the charts.